SPOTLIGHT

D0556693

CALGARY

ANDREW HEMPSTEAD

Contents

CALGARY AND VICINITY

Calgary's nickname, "Cowtown," is cherished by the city's one million residents, who prefer that romantic vision of their beloved home to the city's more modern identity as a world energy and financial center. The city's rapid growth, from a North West Mounted Police (NWMP) post to a large and vibrant metropolis in little more than 100 years, can be credited largely to the effects of resource development, particularly oil and natural gas. Once run by gentlemen who had made their fortunes in ranching, Calgary is still an important cattle market. But a string of oil-and-gas bonanzas changed everything. The natural resources discovered throughout western Canada brought enormous wealth and growth to the city, turning it into the headquarters for a burgeoning energy industry. Downtown is a massive cluster of modern steel-and-glass skyscrapers, the legacy of an explosion of wealth in the 1970s, with cranes once again making their appearance as new commercial projects totaling over $1 billion are currently under construction. Set in this futuristic mirage on the prairie are banks, insurance companies, investment companies, and the head offices of hundreds of oil companies. But not forgetting its roots, each July the city sets aside all the material success it's achieved as a boomtown to put on the greatest outdoor show on earth—the Calgary Stampede, a Western extravaganza second to none.

Calgary is centrally located for a number of interesting yet diverse daytrips. While the vast majority of visitors head west, the Red Deer River Valley, east of Calgary, is one of Alberta's

© ANDREW HEMPSTEAD

HIGHLIGHTS

(Glenbow Museum: One of Canada's finest private museums, the Glenbow is renowned for its coverage of native history, and the new Mavericks display will captivate even non-museum types (page 12).

(Calgary Zoo: Yes, you'll see all the usual suspects (hippos, kangaroos, gorillas), but you'll also find a wide range of Canadian mammals – including some you wouldn't want to meet in the wild (page 17).

(Canada Olympic Park: Follow in the footsteps of Eddie the Eagle and the Jamaican bobsled team at the site of the 1988 Olympic Winter Games (page 17).

(Calgary Stampede: Few cities are associated as closely with a festival as Calgary is with the Stampede, a 10-day, early-July celebration of everything cowboy (page 24).

(Royal Tyrrell Museum: The world's biggest museum devoted entirely to paleontology is *the* place to learn about the importance of Alberta's dinosaur-rich badlands (page 38).

(Dinosaur Provincial Park: You can head out to explore the park yourself, but to really make the most of a visit, plan on joining a guided hike or bus tour (page 42).

(Kanananaskis Country Golf Course: Non-golfers won't be too impressed, but if you do golf and plan on playing just one round in the Calgary area, book a tee time here (page 51).

(Highwood Pass: In Peter Lougheed Provincial Park, you'll find the highest road pass in Canada, one of the only places in Canada where you can drive to an area of alpine meadows (page 52).

(Lacombe Corn Maze: Get lost in this unique family-operated attraction (page 73).

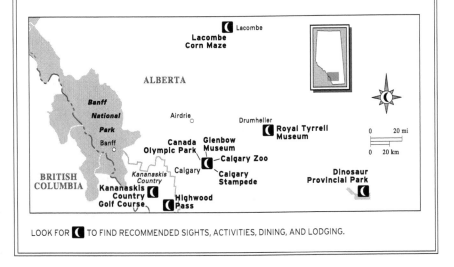

LOOK FOR **(** TO FIND RECOMMENDED SIGHTS, ACTIVITIES, DINING, AND LODGING.

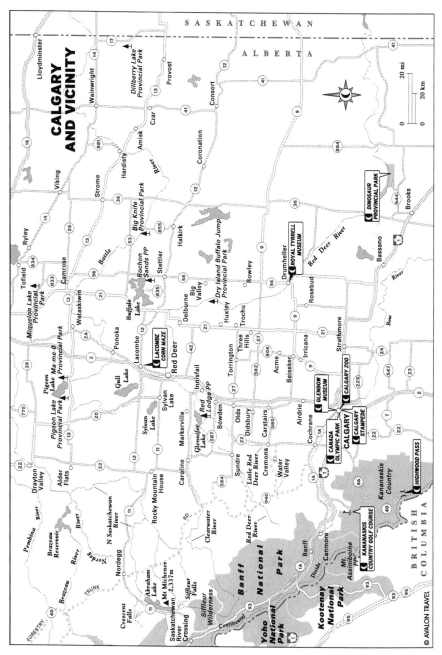

most interesting destinations for one reason: dinosaurs. Here, ancient glacial meltwaters gouged a deep valley into the surrounding rolling prairie, and wind and water have continued the erosion process ever since, all the time uncovering some of the world's premier dinosaur fossil beds. And when you do inevitably turn toward the mountains, there are plenty of reasons to veer from the main highway and explore the southern foothills, which hold some of North America's finest ranching country. Beyond these hills is another reason to delay your arrival in Banff. Known as Kananaskis Country, it is a large tract of mountainous land set aside by the Alberta government as a multiuse recreation area. On the northern edge of Kananaskis Country is the booming mountain town of Canmore, an active outdoor center with a wide array of tourist services. One of the province's busiest roads is Highway 2 through central Alberta between Calgary and Edmonton. This 290-kilometer (180-mile) route takes about three hours to drive straight through, but in the final section of this chapter I'll fill you with ideas for discovering historic towns, exploring scenic parks, and even getting lost (in a corn maze).

PLANNING YOUR TIME

For the vast majority of visitors arriving by air, Calgary International Airport is their first stop in Alberta, and then it's straight off to the mountain national parks of Banff and Jasper. But even with a week in Alberta, it's worth scheduling a day in Calgary—maybe to settle in upon arrival, or to relax the day before flying out—and at least one other to explore the surrounding area. A good first stop to orientate yourself is the top of the Calgary Tower, but attractions such as the Glenbow Museum and Canada Olympic Park should take priority. Another highlight for all ages is the Calgary Zoo, one of the country's best. Attending the Calgary Stampede is a vacation in itself for tens of thousands of visitors each year, but be sure to plan ahead by making accommodation reservations and getting tickets well in advance.

Before charging out in search of dinosaurs,

it is important to understand that the two major attractions, Drumheller's Royal Tyrrell Museum and Dinosaur Provincial Park are separated by a two-hour drive, meaning that if both are visited as a day trip from Calgary, you'll be spending at least five hours on the road. You can include Kananaskis Country and Canmore in your itinerary in a variety of ways, including as a detour between Calgary and Banff, or as a day or overnight trip. Regardless, you won't want to miss the scenery driving over Highwood Pass. Combining the natural attractions of Kananaskis with an afternoon tee time at Kananaskis Country Golf Course would be possible. The route north from Calgary to Edmonton looks straightforward on a map, and the stops you make en route depend mostly on your interests. Those looking for a wilderness experience without the crowds should incorporate the David Thompson Highway into their plan, while those with children will want to stop at the Lacombe Corn Maze.

HISTORY

In addition to being one of Canada's largest cities, Calgary is also one of the youngest; at 140 years old, it has a heritage rather than a history. In 1875 the NWMP established **Fort Calgary** at the confluence of the Bow and Elbow Rivers. It was named after Calgary Bay, a remote Scottish village, with a meaning that is said to translate from Gaelic to "garden on the cove."

The Railway and Ranching

As soon as it was announced that the Canadian Pacific Railway was building its transcontinental railway through Calgary, settlers flooded in. In 1883, a station was built and a townsite was laid out around it. Just nine years after the first train arrived, Calgary acquired city status. In 1886, a fire destroyed most of the town's buildings. City planners decreed that all new structures were to be built of sandstone, which gave the fledgling town a more permanent look. The many sandstone buildings still standing today—the Palliser Hotel, the Hudson's Bay Company store, and the courthouse, for example—are a legacy of this early bylaw.

Fort Calgary was established in 1875.

An open grazing policy, initiated by the Dominion Government, encouraged ranchers in the United States to drive their cattle from overgrazed lands to the fertile plains around Calgary. Slowly, a ranching industry and local beef market developed. The first large ranch was established west of Calgary, and soon many NWMP retirees, English aristocrats, and wealthy American citizens had invested in nearby land.

Oil

In 1914, the discovery of oil at Turner Valley, a short drive southwest of Calgary, signaled the start of an industry that was the making of modern Calgary. The opening of an oil refinery in 1923 and further major discoveries transformed a medium-sized cow town into a world leader in the petroleum and natural gas industries. Calgary became Canada's fastest-growing city, doubling its population between 1950 and 1975; and today, is still Canada's fastest-growing. The population has increased by more than 25 percent since 1996, with current estimates having the city grow another 25 percent to 1.25 million people in the next

decade. Much of the land in and around downtown has been rezoned for multi-family dwellings, with the area south of downtown seeing massive redevelopment and controversial plans in place for the East Village project on the east side of downtown. City limits continue to expand at a phenomenal rate—especially in the northwest, north, and south—with new suburbs, housing estates, and commercial centers extending as far as the eye can see. But Calgary is still a small town at heart, enjoying tremendous civic and public support. Many of the city's self-made millionaires bequeath their money to the city, or, in the case of Glenbow Ranch Provincial Park, deed land for all Calgarians to enjoy. Residents in the thousands are always willing to volunteer their time at events such as the Calgary Stampede. This civic pride makes the city a great place to live and an enjoyable destination for the millions of tourists who visit each year.

ORIENTATION

The TransCanada Highway (Hwy. 1) passes through the city north of downtown and is known as **16th Avenue North** within the city

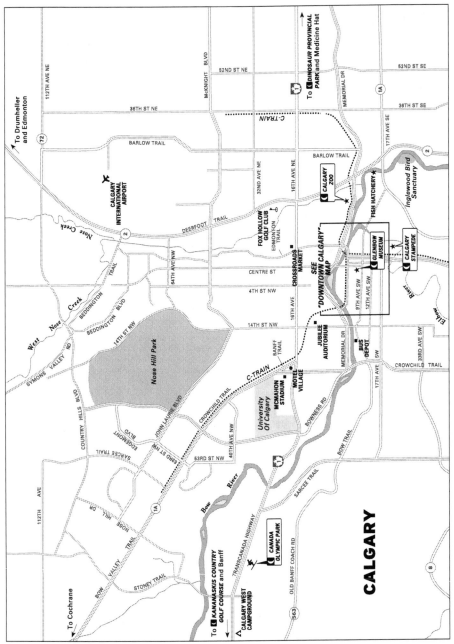

CALGARY

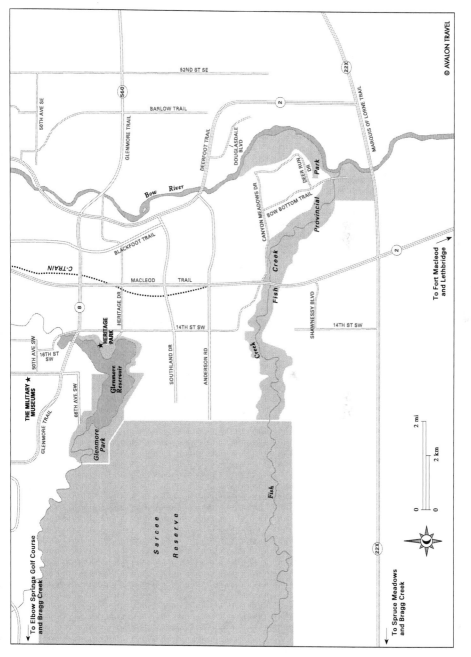

limits. Highway 2, Alberta's major north–south highway, is known as **Deerfoot Trail** within city limits. Many major arteries are known as **trails:** The main route south from downtown is **Macleod Trail,** a 12-kilometer (7.5-mile) strip of malls, motels, restaurants, and retail stores. If you enter Calgary from the west and are heading south, a handy bypass to take is **Sarcee Trail,** then **Glenmore Trail,** which joins Highway 2 south of the city. **Crowchild Trail** starts downtown and heads northwest past the university to Cochrane.

The street-numbering system is divided into four quadrants—northwest, northeast, southwest, and southeast. Each street address has a corresponding abbreviation tacked onto it (NW, NE, SW, and SE). The north–south division is the Bow River. The east–west division is at Macleod Trail and north of downtown at **Centre Street.** Streets run north to south and avenues from east to west. Both streets and avenues are numbered progressively from the quadrant divisions (e.g., an address on 58th Ave. SE is the 58th street south of the Bow River, is east of Macleod Trail, and is on a street that runs east to west).

Sights

DOWNTOWN

The downtown core is a mass of modern steel-and-glass high-tech high-rises, but between the skyscrapers are a number of the city's oldest sandstone buildings. The best place to see these is **Stephen Avenue Walk,** along 8th Avenue between 1st Street SE and 3rd Street SW. This bustling, tree-lined pedestrian mall

Stephen Avenue Walk is a pedestrian-only mall.

also has fountains, benches, cafés, restaurants, and souvenir shops. In summer, the mall is full with shoppers and tourists, and at lunchtime, thousands of office workers descend from the buildings above. At the east end of Stephen Avenue Walk is **Olympic Plaza,** where nightly medal presentations took place during the 1988 Winter Olympic Games. In summer, outdoor concerts are held here, and in winter, the shallow wading pool freezes over and is used as an ice-skating rink. Across 2nd Street SE from the plaza is **City Hall,** built in 1911. It still houses some city offices, although most have moved next door to the modern **Civic Complex.**

Crisscrossing downtown is the **Plus 15** walkway system—a series of interconnecting, enclosed sidewalks elevated at least 4.5 meters (15 feet—hence the name) above road level. In total, 47 bridges and 12 kilometers (7.5 miles) of public walkway link downtown stores, four large malls, hotels, food courts, and office buildings to give pedestrians protection from the elements. All walkways are well marked and wheelchair accessible.

The following sights can be visited separately or seen on a walking tour (in the order presented).

◖ Glenbow Museum

Adjacent to Stephen Avenue Walk, this excellent

CALGARY FOR KIDS

Calgary offers plenty of distractions for children. **Calgary Zoo** and **Heritage Park** (detailed in the main text) mix kid-friendliness with enough of interest to keep grown-ups busy as well. Here are a few other suggestions to keep the young ones occupied.

CREATIVE KIDS MUSEUM/ TELUS WORLD OF SCIENCE

This downtown complex (Mon.-Thurs. 9:30 A.M.-54 P.M., Fri. 9:45 A.M.-5 P.M., the rest of the year Tues Sat.-Sun. 10 A.M.-5 P.M., adult $15, senior $1214.25, child $10) is a wonderful facility chockablock full of interactive exhibits. In the Kids Museum, it's sensory overload in rooms such as Scribble Dee Dee, where young ones hone their painting skills; Sound and Music, with the opportunity to make music; Mindscapes, comprising models of Alberta landscapes that are fully climbable; and Perception, a series of interactive games. In the World of Science section, WOWtown is especially for the under-seven crowd with a working crane model, playground and maze, microscopes, optical illusions, and even a "quiet room." In the **Discovery Dome,** dynamic audiovisuals are projected onto a massive concave screen.

OUT AND ABOUT

Kids will be kids, so plan on taking a break from Calgary's regular attractions and head 10 kilometers (6.2 miles) west of the city limits to **Calaway Park** (TransCanada Hwy., 403/240-3822, Sat.-Sun. 10 A.M.-8 P.M. May-June, daily 10 A.M.-8 P.M. July-Aug., Sat.-Sun. 11 A.M.-6 P.M. Sept.-mid-Oct.), with 27 rides including a double-loop roller coaster. Other attractions include an enormous maze, Western-themed mini-golf, a trout-fishing pond, live entertainment in the Western-style "Showtime Theatre," and many eateries. Admission including most rides is $32 for those aged 7-49, $25 for those aged 3-6 or 50 and over.

The **City of Calgary** (403/268-2489) operates nine outdoor pools (open June-early Sept.) and 12 indoor pools (open year-round). Facilities at each vary. The outdoor pools in **Fish Creek Provincial Park** are among the most popular, while the nearby **Family Leisure Centre** (11150 Bonaventure Dr. SE, 403/278-7542, daily 9 A.M.-9 P.M.) has a lot more to offer than just swimming. Entry of adult $12, child $6 includes use of regular pools as well as a giant indoor water slide, a wave pool, and even a skating rink.

museum (130 9th Ave. SE, 403/268-4100, Mon.–Sat. 9 A.M.–5 P.M., Sun. noon–5 P.M., adult $14, senior $10, child $9) chronicles the entire history of western Canada through three floors of informative exhibits and well-displayed artifacts. The museum's permanent collections of contemporary and Inuit art, as well as special exhibitions from national and international collections, are on the 2nd floor. The 3rd-floor "Niitsitapiisini: Our Way of Life" gallery is the best part of the museum. Developed under the watchful eye of Blackfoot elders, it details the stories and traditions of native peoples through interpretive panels and displays of ceremonial artifacts, jewelry, and a full-size tepee. The Glenbow's renowned library and archives are open Tuesday–Friday 10 A.M.–5 P.M.

Calgary Tower

Cross 9th Avenue from the Glenbow Museum to reach one of the city's most famous landmarks, the Calgary Tower (101 9th Ave., at the corner of Centre St., 403/266-7171, daily 9 A.M.–9 P.M., until 10 P.M. in summer, adult $13, senior $11, child $5). Built in 1968, this 190-meter (620-ft) tower dominated the skyline until 1985, when the nearby Petro-Canada towers went up. Although it's now only Calgary's fourth-tallest building, the ride to the top is a worthwhile introduction to the city. The Observation Terrace affords a bird's-eye view of the Canadian Rockies and the ski-jump towers at Canada Olympic Park to the west; the Olympic Saddledome (in Stampede Park) to the south; and the city below, literally—a glass floor allows visitors to stand right over the

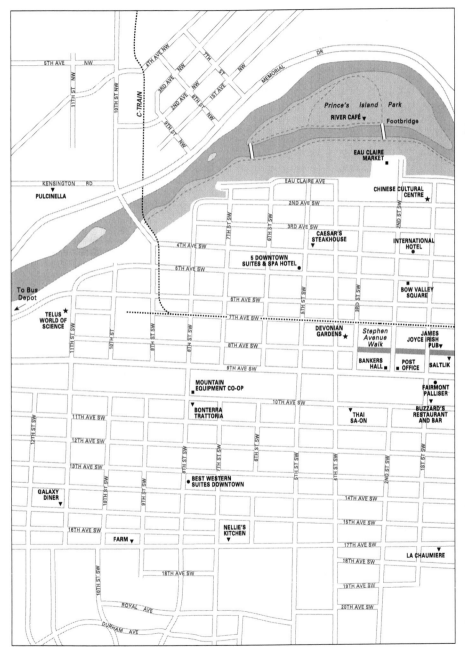

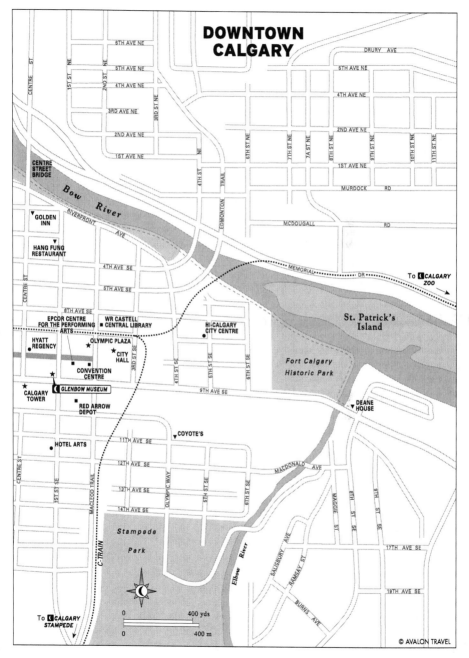

DOWNTOWN CALGARY

top of 9th Avenue. The tower also houses two restaurants, a snack bar, and a gift shop.

Devonian Gardens

A glass-enclosed elevator rises to the 4th floor of Toronto Dominion Square (8th Ave. and 3rd St. SW, 403/221-4274, daily 9 A.M.–9 P.M., free), where a one-hectare (2.5-acre) indoor garden features 16,000 subtropical plants and 4,000 local plants—138 species in all. Within the gardens are waterfalls, fountains, pools, and bridges. Lunchtime entertainers and art exhibits can often be enjoyed in this serene environment.

Chinatown

At the east end of town on 3rd Avenue is a small Chinatown of approximately 2,000 residents. Chinese immigrants came to Calgary in the 1880s to work on the railroads and stayed to establish food markets, restaurants, and import stores. Chinatown has seen its share of prejudice, from marauding whites gaining revenge for an outbreak of smallpox to bungling city bureaucrats who demanded that the streets be narrow and signs be in Chinese to give the area an authentic look. The **Calgary Chinese Cultural Centre** (197 1st St. SW, 403/262-5071, daily 9 A.M.–9 P.M.) is one of the largest such centers in Canada. It's topped by a grand central dome patterned in the same style as the Temple of Heaven in Beijing. The centerpiece of its intricate tile work is a glistening golden dragon hanging 20 meters (66 ft) above the floor. Head up to the 3rd floor for the best views, passing a mural along the way. At street level is a store selling traditional Chinese medicines and on the lower level is a small museum and gallery (daily 11 A.M.–5 P.M., adult $4, senior and child $2) displaying the cultural history of Calgarians of Chinese descent. One of the museum's most intriguing pieces is the world's oldest known seismograph, which dates to A.D. 132.

West on 1st Avenue

Eau Claire Market at the north end of 3rd Street SW is a colorful indoor market filled with stalls selling fresh fruit from British Columbia, seafood from the Pacific, Alberta beef, bakery items, and exotic imports. Under the same roof are specialty shops, an IMAX and regular theaters, and nine restaurants.

The northern limit of downtown is along the Bow River, where picturesque **Prince's Island Park** is linked to the mainland by a bridge at the end of 3rd Street SW. Jogging paths, tables, and grassy areas are scattered among the trees on this man-made island. To the east is **Centre Street Bridge,** guarded on either side by large (restored) stone lions. For a good view of the city, cross the bridge and follow the trail along the cliff to the west.

Telus World of Science

This complex (701 11th St. SW, 403/268-8300, www.calgaryscience.ca, Mon.–Thurs. 9:45 A.M.–4 P.M., Fri. 9:45 A.M.–5 P.M., Sat.–Sun. 10 A.M.–5 P.M., adult $14.25, child $10, includes admission to the Creative Kids Museum) is kid-oriented, but that's not a bad thing. It's a wonderful facility chockablock with hands-on science exhibits. WOWtown is especially for the under-seven crowd—there's a working crane model, playground and maze, microscopes, optical illusions, and even a "quiet room."

Fort Calgary

In 1875, with the onset of a harsh winter, the newly arrived NWMP built Fort Calgary at the confluence of the Bow and Elbow Rivers in less than six weeks. The original fort is long gone, but after much work, the 16-hectare (40-acre) site has been transformed into a two-part historic park (750 9th Ave. SE, 403/290-1875, daily 9 A.M.–5 P.M., adult $11, senior $10, child $5). Most of the focus is on the interpretive center, housing a replica of 1888 barracks, complete with volunteer RCMP veterans on hand to answer questions. Inside, the lives of Canada's famous "Mounties," the legacy of natives, hardy pioneers, and the wild frontier they tamed are all brought to life through convincingly-costumed interpreters. Beside the barracks is an exact replica of the original fort, built using tools and techniques that are more than 100 years old. History comes alive through a variety of activities and programs, including carpenters at work, a room especially for kids that is filled with games of a bygone era, a museum shop styled on an old Hudson's Bay Company store, and a canteen selling meals that I imagine are more appealing than those the original officers enjoyed.

◖ Calgary Zoo

The Calgary Zoo (1300 Zoo Rd. NE, 403/232-9300, year-round daily 9 A.M.–5 P.M., adult $18, senior $16, child $10) is one of Canada's finest zoos. Unique viewing areas have been designed to allow visitors the best look at the zoo's 1,000-plus animals. For example, in Destination Africa, giraffes tower over a huge glass-walled pool that provides a home to two hippos, with sunken stadium seating allowing visitors a fish-eye view of hippos' often-relaxing day. The second "ecosystem" of Destination Africa is a massive building that re-creates a rainforest, with gorillas and monkeys absolutely everywhere. Other highlights include a section on Australia's nocturnal animals, exotic mammals such as lions and tigers, and conservatories filled with tropical flowers, butterflies, and birds. One of the largest display areas is Canadian Wilds, devoted to the mammals you may or may not see on your travels through Alberta. In the Prehistoric Park section, the world of dinosaurs is brought to life with 27 full-size replicas set amid plantlife and rock formations supposedly similar to those found in Alberta in prehistoric times, but looking more like badlands. Nature Tales is a daily interpretive program that takes in everything from trained elephants strutting their stuff to grizzly-bear feeding.

◖ CANADA OLYMPIC PARK

The 1988 Winter Olympic Games are remembered for many things, but particularly a bobsled team from Jamaica, the antics of English plumber/ski-jumper "Eddie the Eagle," and most of all, for their success. This 95-hectare (235-acre) park (403/247-5452, www.

winsportcanada.ca) on the south side of the TransCanada Highway on the western outskirts of the city is the legacy Calgarians get to enjoy year-round. It was developed especially for the Paralympics and the ski-jumping, luge, bobsled, and freestyle skiing events of the games. Now the park offers activities year-round, including tours of the facilities, luge rides, summer ski-jumping, and sports training camps. In winter, the beginner/intermediate runs are filled with locals who are able to hit the snow as early as November with the help of a complex snowmaking system. Many ski-jumping, bobsled, and luge events of national and international standard are held here throughout winter.

Olympic Hall of Fame

This is North America's largest museum devoted to the Olympic Games (mid-May–Sept. daily 10 A.M.–5 P.M., adult $8, child $5.50). Three floors catalog the entire history of the Winter Olympic Games through more than 1,500 exhibits, interactive video displays, costumes and memorabilia, an athletes timeline, a bobsled and ski-jump simulator, and highlights from the last five Winter Olympic Games held at Albertville (France), Lillehammer (Norway), Nagano (Japan), Salt Lake City (United States), and Turin (Italy), including costumes worn by Jamie Sale and David Pelletier during their infamous silver-then-gold-medal-winning final skate.

Ski-Jumping, Luge, and Bobsled Facilities

Visible from throughout the city are the 70- and 90-meter ski-jump towers, synonymous with the Winter Olympic Games. These two jumps are still used for national and international competitions and training. A glass-enclosed elevator rises to the observation level. The jump complex has three additional jumps of 15, 30, and 50 meters, which are used for junior competitions and training. All but the 90-meter jump have plastic-surfaced landing strips and are used during summer.

At the western end of the park are the luge

and bobsled tracks. A complex refrigeration system keeps the tracks usable even on relatively hot days (up to 28 °C/80 °F). At the bottom of the hill is the Ice House, home to the National Sliding Centre, the world's only year-round facility where athletes can practice their dynamic starts for luge, bobsled, and skeleton. Self-guided tours (mid-May–Sept. daily 10 P.M.–5 P.M.) cost $16 per person.

SOUTH OF DOWNTOWN
The Military Museums
Combining former naval and regiments museums, as well as new galleries devoted to the Canadian Air Force, The Military Museums (4520 Crowchild Trail SW, 403/974-2850, Mon.–Fri. 9 A.M.–5 P.M., Sat.–Sun. 9:30 A.M.–4 P.M., adult $6, senior $4, child $3) opened in 2007 as Canada's largest military museum. Highlights include the history of four regiments—Lord Strathcona's Horse Regiment, Princess Patricia's Canadian Light Infantry, the King's Own Calgary Regiment, and the Calgary Highlanders—and the importance of Canada's navy, which was the Allies' third-largest navy in 1945. On display are three fighter aircraft that flew from the decks of aircraft carriers, as well as uniforms, models, flags, photographs, and a memorial to those who lost their lives in the Korean War.

Heritage Park
This 27-hectare (66-acre) park (1900 Heritage Dr. SW, 403/268-8500, mid-May–Aug. daily 10 A.M.–5 P.M., Sept.–early Oct. Sat.–Sun. only 10 A.M.–5 P.M., Gasoline Alley open year-round daily 9:30 A.M.–5 P.M., adult $20, senior $16, child $15, an extra $12 per person for unlimited rides) is on a peninsula jutting into Glenbow Reservoir southwest of downtown. At the entrance is a cobbled courtyard with shops and the excellent Selkirk Grille Restaurant. In the same building as the restaurant is Gasoline Alley, an indoor exhibit open

year round showcasing the history of vehicles. Behind here, more than 100 buildings and exhibits help re-create an early-20th-century pioneer village. Many of the buildings have been moved to the park from their original locations. Highlights include a Hudson's Bay Company fort, a two-story outhouse, a working blacksmith's shop, an 1896 church, a tepee, and an old schoolhouse with original desks. A boardwalk links stores crammed with antiques, and horse-drawn buggies carry passengers along the streets. You can also ride in authentic passenger cars pulled by a steam locomotive or enjoy a cruise in a paddle wheeler on the reservoir. A traditional bakery sells cakes and pastries, and full meals are served in the Wainwright Hotel. To get there from downtown, take the C-train to Heritage Station and transfer to bus #502 (weekends only).

Fish Creek Provincial Park
At the southern edge of the city, this 1,170-hectare (2,900-acre) park is one of the largest urban parks in North America. The site—much of which was once owned by Patrick Burns, the meat magnate—was officially declared a park in 1975. Three geographical regions meet in the area, giving the park a diversity of habitat. Stands of aspen and spruce predominate, but a mixed-grass prairie, as well as balsam, poplar, and willow, can be found along the floodplains at the east end of the park. The ground is colorfully carpeted with 364 recorded species of wildflowers, and wildlife is abundant. Mule, deer, and ground squirrels are common, and white-tailed deer, coyotes, beavers, and the occasional moose are also present. An interpretive trail begins south of Bow Valley Ranch and leads through a grove of balsam and poplar to a shallow, conglomerate cave. The easiest access to the heart of the park is to turn east on Canyon Meadows Drive from Macleod Trail, then south on Bow River Bottom Trail.

Recreation

The **City of Calgary** (403/268-2489, www.calgary.ca) operates a wide variety of recreational facilities, including swimming pools and golf courses, throughout the city. They also run a variety of excursions, such as canoeing and horseback riding, as well as inexpensive courses ranging from fly-tying to rock-climbing.

WALKING AND BIKING

A good way to get a feel for the city is by walking or biking along the 210 kilometers (130 miles) of paved trails within the city limits. The trail system is concentrated along the Bow River as it winds through the city; other options are limited. Along the riverbank, the trail passes through numerous parks and older neighborhoods to various sights such as Fort Calgary and Inglewood Bird Sanctuary. From Fort Calgary, a trail passes under 9th Avenue SE and follows the Elbow River, crossing it several times before ending at Glenmore Reservoir and Heritage Park. Ask at tourist information centers for a map detailing all trails. The ski slopes at **Canada Olympic Park** (west of downtown along the TransCanada Hwy., 403/247-5452) are the perfect place to hone your downhill mountain-bike skills. Full-suspension-bike rental is $40 for two hours or $60 for a full day, while a day pass for the chairlift is $28.

SWIMMING AND FITNESS CENTERS

The **City of Calgary** (403/268-2489) operates eight outdoor pools (open June through early Sept.) and 12 indoor pools (open year-round). Facilities at each vary. Admission at indoor pools includes the use of the sauna, hot tub, and exercise room. Admission to all pools is adult $6.50–9.80, around half price for seniors and kids.

The **YMCA** (101 3rd St. SW, 403/269-6701, Mon.–Fri. 5:30 A.M.–10 P.M., Sat.–Sun. 7 A.M.–7 P.M., $11.90) is a modern fitness center beside Eau Claire Market at the north end of downtown. All facilities are first-class, including an Olympic-size pool, a weight room, an exercise room, a jogging track, squash courts, a hot tub, and a sauna.

TOURS

Brewster (403/221-8242, www.brewster.ca) runs a Calgary City Sights tour lasting four hours. Included on the itinerary are downtown, various historic buildings, Canada Olympic Park, and Fort Calgary. The tours run June through September and cost adult $53, child $27. Pickups are at most major hotels. Brewster also runs day tours departing Calgary daily to Banff, Lake Louise, and the Columbia Icefield. The latter is a grueling 15-hour trip that departs at 6 A.M. Brewster's downtown office is located on Stephen Avenue Walk at the corner of Centre Street.

AMUSEMENT PARKS

Calaway Park (10 km/6.2 mi west of city limits along the TransCanada Hwy., 403/240-3822, May–June Sat.–Sun. 10 A.M.–7 P.M., July–Aug. daily 10 A.M.–7 P.M., Sept.–mid-Oct. Sat.–Sun. 11 A.M.–6 P.M.) is western Canada's largest outdoor amusement park, with 27 rides including a double-loop roller coaster. Other attractions include an enormous maze, Western-themed mini-golf, a zoo for the kids, a trout-fishing pond, live entertainment in the Western-style "Showtime Theatre," and many eateries. Admission including most rides is $32 for those aged 7–49, $25 for those aged 3–6 and 50 and over.

WINTER RECREATION

When Calgarians talk about going skiing or snowboarding for the day, they are usually referring to the five world-class winter resorts in the Rockies, a one- to two-hour drive to the west. The city's only downhill facilities are at **Canada Olympic Park** (403/247-5452), which has three chairlifts and a T-bar serving a vertical rise of 150 meters (500 ft). Although the slopes aren't extensive, on the plus side are a long season (mid-Nov. to late March), night skiing (weeknights until 9 P.M.), extensive lodge facilities including rentals, and excellent teaching staff. Lift tickets can be purchased on an hourly basis ($28 for four hours) or for a full day ($38). Seniors pay just $16 for a full day on the slopes.

SPECTATOR SPORTS

There's no better way to spend a winter's night in Calgary than by attending a home game of the **Calgary Flames** (403/777-2177, www.calgaryflames.com), the city's National Hockey League franchise. The regular season runs October–April, and home games are usually held in the early evening.

The **Stampeders** (403/289-0205, www.stampeders.com) are Calgary's franchise in the Canadian Football League (CFL), an organization similar to the American NFL. The season runs July–November. Home games are played at the 35,500-seat **McMahon Stadium** (1817 Crowchild Trail NW). From downtown, take the C-train to Banff Trail Station. Tickets range $29–89.

Spruce Meadows

It is somewhat ironic that a city known around the world for its rodeo is also home to the world's premier show-jumping facility, **Spruce Meadows** (Spruce Meadows Way, 403/974-4200, www.sprucemeadows.com). Ever-encroaching residential developments do nothing to take away from the wonderfully refined atmosphere within the white picket fence that surrounds the sprawling 120-hectare (300-acre) site. The facility comprises 6 grassed outdoor rings, 2 indoor arenas, 7 stables holding 700 horse stalls, 90 full-time employees (and many thousands of volunteers), and its own television station that broadcasts to 90 countries.

Spruce Meadows hosts a packed schedule of tournaments that attract the world's best riders and up to 50,000 spectators a day. The four big tournaments are the **National,** the first week of June; **Canada One,** the last week of June; the **North American,** the first week of July; and the **Masters,** the first week of September. The Masters is the world's richest show-jumping tournament, with one million dollars up for grabs on the Sunday afternoon ride-off.

Enjoy the traditions of show-jumping at Spruce Meadows.

© ANDREW HEMPSTEAD

General admission is free. Except on the busiest of days, this will get you a prime viewing position at any of the rings. The exception is tournament weekends, when covered reserved seating ($25–35) is the best way to watch the action. To get to Spruce Meadows on tournament weekends, take C-train south to Fish Creek–Lacombe Station, from which bus transfers to the grounds are free. By car, take Macleod Trail south to Highway 22X and turn right toward the mountains along Spruce Meadows Way.

Arts, Entertainment, and Shopping

ffwd (www.ffwdweekly.com) is a free weekly magazine available throughout the city. It lists theater events, cinema screenings, and art displays, and keeps everyone abreast of the local music scene. Tickets to major concerts, performances, and sporting events are available in advance from **Ticketmaster** (403/777-0000, www.ticketmaster.ca).

THE ARTS
Art Galleries
It may put a dent in Calgary's cow town image, but the city does have a remarkable number of galleries displaying and selling work by Albertan and Canadian artisans. Unfortunately, they are not concentrated in any one area, and most require some effort to find. Renowned for its authentic native art, **Micah Gallery** is the exception. It's right downtown on Stephen Avenue Walk (110 8th Ave. SW, 403/245-1340). A cluster of galleries lies along 9th Avenue SE. Most affordable is **Galleria Arts & Crafts** (907 9th Ave. SE., 403/270-3612), with two stories of shelf space stocked with paintings, etchings, metal sculptures, jewelry, and wood carvings. Here also, **The Collectors Gallery** (1332 9th Ave. SE, 403/245-8300) sells the work of prominent 19th- and 20th-century Canadian artists.

Theater
Calgary's Western image belies a cultural diversity that goes further than being able to get a few foreign beers at the local saloon. In fact, the city has 10 professional theater companies, an opera, an orchestra, and a ballet troupe. The main season for performances is September–May.

Alberta Theatre Projects (403/294-7402, www.atplive.com) is a well-established company based in the downtown Epcor Centre for the Performing Arts (220 9th Ave. SE). Usual performances are of contemporary material. Expect to pay under $20 for matinees and up to $66 for the very best evening seats. Also based at the Epcor Centre for the Performing Arts is **Theatre Calgary** (403/294-7440, www.theatrecalgary.com). **Lunchbox Theatre** (115 9th Ave. SE, 403/265-4292, www.lunchboxtheatre.com), in a custom-built theater at the base of the Calgary Tower, runs especially for the lunchtime crowd from September to early May. Adults pay $18, seniors $15 for usually comedic content. For adult-oriented experimental productions, consider a performance by **One Yellow Rabbit** (Epcor Centre for the Performing Arts, 403/264-3224, www.oyr.org).

Music and Dance
Calgary Opera (403/262-7286, www.calgaryopera.com) performs in a restored church (corner 13th Ave. and 7th St. SW) October–April. Tickets range $22–88. The 2,000-seat Jack Singer Concert Hall at the Epcor Centre for the Performing Arts is home to the **Calgary Philharmonic Orchestra** (403/571-0270, www.cpo-live.com), one of Canada's top orchestras. **Alberta Ballet** (403/245-4549, www.albertaballet.com) performs at locations throughout the city.

Cinemas
Many major shopping malls—including Eau Claire Market, closest to downtown—have a **Cineplex** cinema. For information, call the 24-hour film line (403/263-3166) or check the

website (www.cineplex.com). **Uptown Stage & Screen** (610 8th Ave. SW, 403/265-0120, www.theuptown.com) is a restored downtown theater that has a reputation for alternative, art, and foreign films. Over the Bow River from downtown, the 1935 **Plaza Theatre** (1133 Kensington Rd. NW, Kensington, 403/283-2222, www.theplaza.ca) shows everything from mainstream to Hindi.

NIGHTLIFE
Bars and Nightclubs
With a nickname like Cowtown it's not surprising that some of Calgary's hottest nightspots play country music. **Ranchman's** (9615 Macleod Trail SW, 403/253-1100) is *the* place to check out first, especially during Stampede Week. Some of country's hottest stars have played this authentic honky-tonk. Food is served at a bar out front all day, then at 7 P.M. the large dance hall opens with a band keeping the crowd boot-scootin' most nights. The hall is a museum of rodeo memorabilia and photographs, with a chuck wagon hanging from the ceiling. On the south side of the railway tracks from downtown, is hip **Cowboys** (1088 Olympic Way SE, 403/265-0699). The crowd is urban-slick, but when country music plays, the fancy-dancing crowd seems to know every word.

Options for a quiet drink in a refined setting include lounge bars in major downtown hotels. Of these, the **Sandstone Lounge** (Hyatt Regency, 700 Centre St., 403/717-1234) stands out for its central location (off Stephen Avenue Walk), classy surroundings, and extensive drink selection. **Raw Bar** (Hotel Arts, 119 12th Ave. SW, 403/266-4611, daily 11 A.M.–9 P.M.) is as exotic as it gets in Calgary—a cabana-like setting around an outdoor pool. Back on Stephen Avenue Walk, in an old bank building, **James Joyce Irish Pub** (114 8th Ave. SW, 403/262-0708) has Guinness on tap and a menu of traditional British dishes.

If you're looking to dance the night away (without doing it in a line), there's a number of non-country alternatives. Downtown in a grandly restored theater, **The Palace** (218 8th Ave. SW, 403/263-9980) has a large dance floor and big-time lighting and sound systems. **Mercury Lounge** (550 17th Ave. SW, 403/229-0222) attracts a young, hip crowd for its cocktail-bar ambience—the perfect pre-nightclub hangout. For many Mercury patrons, the next stop is **Tequila** (219 17th Ave. SW, 403/209-2215), where a DJ spins house and hip-hop for a young party crowd. Also within walking distance is the **Metropolitan Grill** (880 16th Ave. SW, 403/802-2393), where the over-25 crowd gravitates to the outdoor patio on warm summer nights. Glitzy **Tantra** (355 10th Ave. SW, 403/264-0202) attracts the beautiful, high-end crowd, but remains welcoming.

Jazz and Blues
The days of Buddy Guy and Junior Wells taking to the stage of the venerable King Edward Hotel are just a memory, but a couple of modern venues attract jazz and blues enthusiasts. One of the most popular jazz clubs in town is **Beat Niq** (at the lower level of 811 1st St., 403/263-1650), a New York–style jazz club that welcomes everyone. It's open Thursday–Saturday from 8 P.M. and the cover charge is $12–18.

SHOPPING
Plazas and Malls
The largest shopping center downtown is **Calgary Eaton Centre,** on Stephen Avenue Walk at 4th Street SW. This center is linked to other plazas by the Plus 15 Walkway System. Other downtown shopping complexes are **Eau Claire Market,** at the entrance to Prince's Island Park, where the emphasis is on fresh foods and trendy boutiques; **TD Square,** at 7th Avenue and 2nd Street SW; and **The Bay,** part of Alberta's history with its link to the Hudson's Bay Company. **Uptown 17** is a strip of more than 400 retail shops, restaurants, and galleries along 17th Avenue SW. **Kensington,** across the Bow River from downtown, is an eclectic mix of specialty shops.

Markets
At **Crossroads Market** (1235 26th Ave. SE,

403/291-5208, Fri.–Sun. 9 A.M.–5 P.M.) you'll find rows and rows of local seasonal produce as well as prepared foods like the well-researched Simple Simon Pies. Crossroads is also known for its arts and crafts.

Camping Gear and Western Wear

Mountain Equipment Co-op (830 10th Ave. SW, 403/269-2420) is Calgary's largest camping store. This massive outlet boasts an extensive range of high-quality clothing, climbing and mountaineering equipment (including a climbing wall), tents, sleeping bags, kayaks and canoes, books and maps, and other accessories. The store is a cooperative owned by its members, similar to the American REI stores, except that to purchase anything you must be a member (a once-only $5 charge).

Alberta Boot Co. (614 10th Ave. SW, 403/263-4605), within walking distance of downtown, is Alberta's only Western-boot manufacturer. This outlet shop has thousands of pairs for sale in all shapes and sizes, all made from leather. Boots start at $250 and go all the way up to $1,700 for alligator hide. You'll find **Lammle's Western Wear** outlets in all the major malls and downtown on Stephen Avenue Walk. Another popular Western outfitter is **Riley & McCormick,** also on Stephen Avenue Walk (220 8th Ave. SW, 403/262-1556) and at the airport.

Bookstores

For topographic, city, and wall maps, as well as travel guides and atlases, **Map Town** (400 5th Ave. SW, 403/266-2241 or 877/921-6277, www.maptown.com, Mon.–Fri. 9 A.M.–6 P.M., Sat. 10 A.M.–5 P.M.) should have what you're looking for. Tech-savvy travelers will be impressed by the selection of GPS units and related software, as well as the scanning service, which allows you to have topo maps sent directly to your email inbox.

The suburb of Kensington, immediately northwest of downtown, is home to **Pages** (1135 Kensington Rd. NW, 403/283-6655, Mon.–Sat. 10 A.M.–5:30 P.M., Thurs.–Fri. until 9 P.M., and Sun. noon–5 P.M.), which offers a thoughtful selection of Canadian fiction and nonfiction titles.

Fair's Fair (1609 14th St. SW, 403/245-2778, daily from 10 A.M.) is the biggest of Calgary's secondhand and collector bookstores. Surprise, surprise, it's remarkably well organized, with a solid collection of well-labeled Canadiana filling more than one room. Fair's Fair has another large outlet in Inglewood (907 9th Ave. SE, 403/237-8156). On the north side of downtown, **Aquila Books** (826 16th Ave. NW, 403/282-5832) is a real gem, with one of the world's best collections of antiquarian Canadian Rockies and mountaineering books.

Festivals and Events

SPRING

Calgary International Children's Festival (403/294-7414, www.calgarychildfest.org) is the third week of May. Events include theater, puppetry, and performances by musicians from around the world. It's held in the Epcor Centre for the Performing Arts and Olympic Plaza. Olympic Plaza comes alive with the sights, sounds, and tastes of the Caribbean on the second Saturday of June for **Carifest** (403/774-1300, www.carifestcalgary.ca).

SUMMER

Few cities in the world are associated as closely with an event as Calgary is with the **Calgary Stampede.** For details of the "Greatest Outdoor Show on Earth," held each summer in July, see *Calgary Stampede* later in this section.

Canada Day is celebrated on July 1 in Prince's Island Park, Fort Calgary, the zoo, and Heritage Park. The **Calgary Folk Music Festival** (403/233-0904, www.calgaryfolkfest.

com), during the last weekend of July, is an indoor and outdoor extravaganza of Canadian and international performers that centers on Prince's Island Park. The first full week of August, and also at this downtown riverfront park, is **Afrikadey!** (403/234-9110, www.afrikadey.com), with performances and workshops by African-influenced musicians and artists and screenings of African-themed films.

FALL

In October, **hockey** and **skiing and snowboarding** fever hits the city as the **NHL Calgary Flames** start their season and the first snow flies. Late September through early October sees screenings of movies during the **Calgary International Film Festival** (403/283-1490, www.calgaryfilm.com) at the historic Plaza theater, and at the Globe Theatre and Cineplex at Eau Claire Market. This is followed by **Wordfest** (403/237-9068, www.wordfest.com), where authors talk about their books, workshops are given, and many readings

take place at venues throughout the city and in Banff. As Halloween approaches a good place for kids is Calgary Zoo (403/232-9300, www.calgaryzoo.org), where there are **Boo at the Zoo** celebrations after dark throughout the last week of October.

WINTER

Calgary has joined other major Canadian cities by celebrating New Year's Eve with a **First Night** festival. Although severely curtailed by the weather, Calgarians enjoy the winter with the opening of the theater, ballet, and opera seasons. National and international ski-jumping, luge, and bobsledding events are held at **Canada Olympic Park** November–March.

◖ CALGARY STAMPEDE

Every July since 1912, the city's perennial rough-and-ready cow town image has been thrust to the forefront when a fever known as Stampede hits town. For 10 days, Calgarians let their hair down—business leaders don Stetsons, bankers wear boots, half the town

The Calgary Stampede is western Canada's best-known event.

walks around in too-tight denim outfits, and the rate of serious crime drops. Nine months later, maternity hospitals report a rise in business. For most Calgarians, it is known simply as The Week (always capitalized). The Stampede is many things to many people but is certainly not for the cynic. It is a celebration of the city's past—of endless sunny days when life was broncos, bulls, and steers, of cowboys riding through the streets, and saloons on every corner. But it is not just about the past. It's the cow town image Calgarians cherish, and the frontier image that visitors expect. On downtown streets, everyone is your neighbor. Flapjacks and bacon are served free of charge around the city; normally staid citizens shout "Ya-HOO!" for no particular reason; Indians ride up and down the streets on horseback; and there's drinking and dancing until dawn every night.

The epicenter of the action is **Stampede Park,** immediately south of the city center, where more than 100,000 people converge each day. The nucleus of the Stampede, the park hosts the world's richest outdoor rodeo and the just-as-spectacular chuck wagon races, where professional cowboys from all over the planet compete to share $1.6 million over 10 days. But Stampede Park offers a lot more than a show of cowboy skills. The gigantic midway takes at least a day to get around: a staggering number of attractions, displays, and free entertainment cost only the price of gate admission; and a glittering grandstand show, complete with fireworks, ends each day's shenanigans.

Stampede Parade

Although Stampede Park opens on Thursday evening for **Sneak-a-Peek** (an event that alone attracts approximately 40,000 eager patrons), Stampede Week officially begins Friday morning with a spectacular parade through the streets of downtown Calgary. The approximately 150 parade participants include close to 4,000 people and 700 horses, and the procession takes two hours to pass any one point. It features an amazing array of floats, each cheered by the 250,000 people who line the streets up to 10 deep. The loudest "Ya-

HOOs" are usually reserved for Alberta's oldest residents, Stampede royalty, and members of Calgary's professional sports teams; but this is the Stampede, so even politicians and street sweepers elicit enthusiastic cheers.

Rodeo

The pinnacle of any cowboy's career is walking away with the $100,000 winner's check on the last day of competition in the Calgary Stampede. For the first 8 days, 20 of the world's best cowboys and cowgirls compete in 2 pools for the right to ride on the final Sunday. Saturday is a wildcard event. On each of the 10 days, the rodeo starts at 1:30 P.M. Although Stampede Week is about a lot more than the rodeo, everyone loves to watch this event. Cowboys compete in bronc riding, bareback riding, bull riding, calf roping, and steer wrestling, and cowgirls compete in barrel racing. Bull fighting and nonstop chatter from hilarious rodeo clowns all keep the action going between the more traditional rodeo events.

Chuck Wagon Races

The **Rangeland Derby** chuck wagon races feature nine heats each evening starting at 8 P.M. At the end of the week, the top four drivers from the preliminary rounds compete in a $100,000 dash-for-the-cash final. Chuck wagon racing is an exciting sport any time, but at the Stampede the pressure is intense as drivers push themselves to stay in the running. The grandstand in the infield makes steering the chuck wagons through an initial figure eight difficult, heightening the action before they burst onto the track for what is known as the Half Mile of Hell to the finish line. The first team across the finish line does not always win the race; drivers must avoid 34 penalties, ranging from 1 to 10 seconds, which are added to their overall time.

Other Highlights

Agricultural displays are situated in the center of Stampede Park. **Centennial Fair** is an outdoor stage with children's attractions such as duck races and magicians. In the **Agricultural**

Building livestock is displayed, and the World Blacksmith's Competition and horse shows take place next door in the **John Deere Show Ring.**

At the far end of Stampede Park, across the Elbow River, is **Indian Village.** Here, members of the five nations who signed Treaty Seven 100 years ago—the Blackfoot, Blood, Piegan, Sarcee, and Stoney—set up camp for the duration of the Stampede. Each tepee has its own colorful design. Behind the village is a stage where native dance competitions are held.

Once you've paid gate admission, all entertainment (except the rodeo and chuck wagon races) is free. Well-known Canadian performers appear at the outdoor **Coca-Cola Stage** from 11 A.M. to midnight. **Nashville North** is an indoor venue with a bar, live country acts, and a dance floor; open until 2 A.M.

Tickets

Advance tickets for the afternoon rodeos and evening chuck wagon races/grandstand shows go on sale the year before the event (usually sometime in September), with the best seats selling out well in advance. The best views are from the "A" section, closest to the infield yet high enough not to miss all the action. Ticket prices for the first eight days of rodeo competition range $35–75 ($56 for section A). The evening chuck wagon races/grandstand shows run $42–84 ($72 for section A). Tickets to both the rodeos and chuck wagon races/grandstand shows include admission to Stampede Park. Order tickets by phone (403/269-9822 or 800/661-1767) or online (www.calgarystampede.com).

If you didn't purchase your tickets in advance, you'll need to pay the $14 **general admission** at the gate. Then, once on the grounds, you can purchase "rush seating" tickets for the afternoon's rodeo (adult $15, child $8) or the chuck wagon race/grandstand show (adult $20, child $12). You'll only have access to either an area of the infield with poor views or seats well away from the action.

Information

Check either of Calgary's daily newspapers for a pull-out section with results of the previous day's competition and a schedule of events on the grounds and around town. At Stampede Park, a schedule and maps are available at distinctive **Howdy Folk Chuckwagons** topped with cowboy hats and staffed by friendly volunteers.

For future dates for the Calgary Stampede, contact the Calgary Stampede office at 403/261-0101 or 800/661-1260, www.calgarystampede.com.

Accommodations and Camping

Accommodations in Calgary vary from campgrounds, a hostel, and budget motels to a broad selection of high-quality hotels catering to top-end travelers and business conventions. During Stampede Week, prices are higher than the rest of the year and accommodations are booked months in advance. Rates quoted below are for a double room in summer, but outside of Stampede week.

The bed-and-breakfast scene in Calgary is alive and well. Most are located off the main tourist routes. The **Bed & Breakfast Association of Calgary** (www.bbcalgary.com) represents around 40 of these homes offering rooms to visitors.

DOWNTOWN
Under $50

Part of the worldwide Hostelling International organization, **HI-Calgary City Centre** (520 7th Avenue SE, 403/670-7580 or 888/762-4122, www.hihostels.ca) is an excellent choice for budget travelers, both for its convenient location and wide variety of facilities. It has 94 beds, most in eight-bed dormitories, but there are a couple of private rooms. Other amenities include a fully equipped kitchen, laundry facilities, a large common room, Internet kiosks, free wireless Internet, bike rental, an outdoor barbecue, a game room, a snack bar, lockers, and free parking. Members of Hostelling International pay $29.50 for a dorm bed ($33 for nonmembers) or $73–79.50 s or d ($81–87.50 for nonmembers) in the private rooms. It's one block east of the City Hall C-train station.

$50-100

The most central bed-and-breakfast is **Inglewood B&B** (1006 8th Ave. SE, 403/262-6570, www.inglewoodbedandbreakfast.com, $100–165 s or d), named for the historic neighborhood in which it lies. Its location is excellent—close to the river and Stampede Park, as well as a 10-minute stroll from downtown. The three rooms within this modern Victorian-style home each have private bathrooms and rates include a cooked breakfast of your own choosing.

$150-200

A few blocks west of the downtown shopping district, but linked by the C-train, you'll find the 301-room **Sandman Hotel** (888 7th Ave. SW, 403/237-8626 or 800/726-3626, www.sandmanhotels.com, $169–235 s or d). This full-service property features an indoor pool, a family-style restaurant, and large, attractive rooms. Pay under $130 through the website.

Least expensive of the hotels right downtown is the **5 Downtown Suites & Spa** (618 5th Ave. SW, 403/451-5551 or 888/561-7666, www.5calgary.com, $159–199). Although the 300 rooms are unremarkable, bonuses include full kitchens, free weekend parking, a free business center, spa services, a restaurant and lounge, and a small outdoor pool.

$200-250

Hotel Arts (119 12th Ave. SW, 403/266-4611 or 800/661-9378, www.hotelarts.ca, $249–436 s or d) is a newish 12-story, 188-room accommodation on the south side of the railway tracks, within easy walking distance

of Stampede Park. The rooms are contemporary-slick, with 42-inch LCD flat-screen TVs, cordless phones, high-speed Internet access, luxurious bathrooms, and plush beds with goose-down duvets. Downstairs is a fitness room, an outdoor heated pool surrounded by a beautiful patio, a restaurant, and a lounge.

The **International Hotel of Calgary** (220 4th Ave. SW, 403/265-9600 or 800/661-8627, www.internationalhotel.ca, $239–289 s or d) features 250 spacious one- and two-bedroom suites, an indoor pool, a fitness room, and a restaurant.

$250-300

When I spend the night in Calgary on business I try to stay somewhere different every time (in the name of research). But when it's a special occasion, it's difficult to beat the **Kensington Riverside Inn** (1126 Memorial Dr. NW, Kensington, 403/228-4442 or 877/313-3733, www.kensingtonriversideinn.com, $299–369 s or d includes breakfast). Why? From the

Kensington Riverside Inn

moment I'm tempted by a homemade cookie from the jar at the reception to the moment I slide between the Egyptian cotton sheets that top ultra-comfortable mattresses, the inn has a captivating atmosphere that is unlike any other city accommodation. Each of the 19 guest rooms has a slightly different feel (from bold contemporary to warmly inviting), but it's in-room niceties such as heated towel racks, or a quiet hour spent in the central living room with evening hors d'oeuvres, that make the inn super special.

Over $300

One block north from the Calgary Tower is the ❦ **Hyatt Regency Calgary** (700 Centre St., 403/717-1234 or 800/492-8804, www.calgary. hyatt.com, $339–429 s or d). Incorporating a historic building along Stephen Avenue Walk in its construction, this 21-story hotel features an indoor swimming pool, a refined lounge, and a renowned restaurant specializing in Canadian cuisine. The hotel's Stillwater Spa is the premier spa facility in Calgary—spend any time here and you'll forget you're in a city

hotel. The up-to-date guest rooms won't take your breath away, but they have a wide range of amenities and luxurious bathrooms.

In the heart of the shopping district, the **Westin Hotel** (320 4th Ave. SW, 403/266-1611 or 888/625-5144, www.westincalgary.com, $419–489 s or d) has a wide range of facilities, including a rooftop indoor swimming pool, a café, the renowned Owl's Nest Restaurant, a lounge, and more than 500 rooms.

Easily Calgary's best-known hotel, the gracious **Fairmont Palliser** (133 9th Ave. SE, 403/263-0520 or 866/540-4477, www.fairmont.com, from $529 s or d) was built in 1914 by the Canadian Pacific Railway for the same clientele as the company's famous properties in Banff and Jasper. The rooms may seem smallish by modern standards, and the hotel lacks certain recreational facilities, but the elegance and character of the grande dame of Calgary accommodations are priceless. The cavernous lobby has original marble columns and staircases, a magnificent chandelier, and solid-brass doors that open onto busy 9th Avenue. As you'd expect, staying at

The Hyatt Regency Calgary rises above downtown.

the Palliser isn't cheap, but it's a luxurious way to enjoy the city.

MACLEOD TRAIL

A string of hotels along Macleod Trail south of downtown picks up highway traffic as it enters the city. Most mid-priced chains are represented, with the following being just a sampling.

$100-150

Most of the chain motels along Macleod Trail fall into this price category. Book in advance or online to pick up rates around $100 a night.

Southernmost of the motels on Macleod Trail is the 34-room **Stetson Village Inn** (10002 Macleod Trail SW, 403/271-3210 or 888/322-3210, www.stetsoninn.ca, $111 s or d), an older-style place tucked between shopping malls.

The **Best Western Calgary Centre Inn** (3630 Macleod Trail SW, 403/287-3900 or 877/287-3900, www.bwcalgarycentre.com, $149–159 s or d) may be close to the geographical center of the city, but it's not downtown as the name suggests. Each of the rooms is decorated in a bright and breezy color scheme, and comes stocked with amenities such as a hair dryer and coffeemaker. On the premises are an indoor pool and a fitness center.

A few blocks farther south, with a C-train station on its back doorstep, stands **Holiday Inn Macleod Trail** (4206 Macleod Trail SW, 403/287-2700 or 800/661-1889, www.holiday-inn.com, $149 s or d), where the 150 rooms were last renovated in 2009. Facilities here include a large indoor pool, a restaurant, and a lounge.

WEST OF DOWNTOWN
$100-150

Motel Village is Calgary's main concentration of moderately priced motels. The "village" is not an official designation, just a dozen motels bunched together on a single block bordered by 16th Avenue NW, Crowchild Trail, and Banff Trail. From the adjacent Banff Trail station, downtown is a short, safe ride away on the C-train. Here, the **C Comfort Inn** (2369 Banff Trail NW, 403/289-2581 or 800/228-5150, www.comfortinncalgary.com, $139–179 s or d includes breakfast) combines a wide range of amenities with reasonable rates to be my pick of Motel Village accommodations. All rooms have a simple yet snazzy contemporary look, along with high-speed Internet, a coffeemaker, a hair dryer, and an ironing facility. Other features include an indoor pool and waterslide complex.

Tucked away on the forested Paskapoo Slopes, beside Canada Olympic Park, **C Ridge Side Retreat** (430 85th St. SW, 403/288-3415 or 877/344-3400, www.ripleyridge.com, $145–375 s or d includes breakfast) offers guests the choice of accommodations in two rustic cabins—one with a full kitchen, the other with a woodstove and loft—or in spacious, comfortable units such as the City Light Suite, which features panoramic city views from a private sitting room.

$150-200

Directly opposite Canada Olympic Park is the **Four Points by Sheraton Calgary West** (8220 Bow Ridge Crescent NW, 403/288-4441 or 877/288-4441, www.fourpointscalgarywest.com, $169–195 s or d), a real standout for motel accommodations on this side of the city. The 150 rooms are big and bright and each has a balcony (ask for one with a view of Canada Olympic Park). Along with city-hotel luxuries like free wireless Internet and room service, other amenities include an indoor pool and water slide, a fitness center, a day spa, and a restaurant.

Across the road from the Sheraton is **Sandman Hotel & Suites** (125 Bow Ridge Crescent NW, 403/288-6033 or 800/726-3626, www.sandmanhotels.com, $185 s or d). It features spacious modern rooms, an indoor pool, a fitness room, and a 24-hour Denny's restaurant.

NORTHEAST (DOWNTOWN)

Many hotels lie in the northeast section of the city at varying distances from Calgary International

Airport. All of those detailed below have airport shuttles, and most can be contacted directly by courtesy phone from the airport.

$100-150

Check hotel websites listed below for rooms around the $100 mark, or take the easy way out and book your stay at the no-frills **Pointe Inn** (1808 19th St. NE, 403/291-4681 or 800/661-8164, www.pointeinn.com, $100–115 s or d). Facilities include a launderette, a restaurant, and a lounge. Request a nonsmoking room.

$150-200

Holiday Inn Calgary Airport (1250 McKinnon Dr. NE, 403/230-1999 or 800/465-4329, www.holidayinn.com, $160–190 s or d) is a little farther from the airport than the other choices, but since there's a free shuttle that is of little consequence. The smallish indoor pool is the perfect place to refresh yourself after a long flight.

Similarly priced is the **Radisson Hotel Calgary Airport** (2120 16th Ave. NE, 403/291-4666 or 800/395-7046, www.radisson.com, $160–260 s or d), which features 185 comfortable rooms, an indoor pool, a fitness center, spa services, and a Western-style saloon. Upgrade to a Business Class room ($180) and enjoy better views, an evening turndown service, and breakfast.

Not right at the airport but of a similarly high standard to the Delta Calgary Airport is the **Sheraton Cavalier** (2620 32nd Ave. NE, 403/291-0107 or 866/716-8101, www.sheratoncavalier.com, $180–265 s or d). This full-service hostelry boasts a variety of dining options, a lounge, a fitness room, an indoor water park, and a business center. The 306 rooms are modern, spacious, and equipped with wireless Internet.

Over $200

☾ Delta Calgary Airport (403/291-2600 or 888/492-8804, www.deltahotels.com, $219 s or d) is the only accommodation right at the airport. The medium-sized rooms come with luxuries like down duvets and plush bathrobes,

each has a writing desk, and most importantly, they are well sound-proofed. Premier Rooms, which are the same size as regular rooms, come with upgraded furnishings for a few bucks extra. Hotel amenities include two restaurants, a lounge, an indoor pool, and a business center.

CAMPING

No camping is available within the Calgary city limits, although campgrounds can be found along all major routes into the city. Shuttle buses run to and from campgrounds into Stampede Park during the Calgary Stampede.

West

The only Calgary campground with an outdoor swimming pool is **☾ Calgary West Campground** (221 101st St. SW, 403/288-0411 or 888/562-0842, www.calgarycampground.com, mid-Apr.–mid-Oct., unserviced sites $32, hookups $39–43), on a north-facing hill a short way west of Canada Olympic Park. In addition to the pool, modern facilities include showers, a laundry room, a game room, and a grocery store. Around 320 sites are laid out on terraces, so no one misses out on the views.

Calaway Park (10 km/6.2 mi west of city limits, 403/249-7372, www.calawaypark.com, mid-May–Aug., tent sites $24, hookups $29–35) is farther out along the TransCanada Highway. It offers a large, open camping area. Trees are scarce, but on clear days the view of the Canadian Rockies is spectacular.

North

Whispering Spruce Campground (403/226-0097, www.whisperingspruce.com, Apr.–Oct., tent sites $24, hookups $26–28) is on the west side of Highway 2, 10 kilometers (6.2 mi) north of the airport. Facilities include showers, a small grocery store, laundry, a game room, and horseshoe pits.

East

Mountainview Farm Campground, three kilometers (1.9 mi) east of the city limits on the

TransCanada Highway (403/293-6640, www. calgarycamping.com, tent sites $31, hookups $35–40) doesn't have a view of the mountains, but it does have mini-golf and hay rides. The sites are very close together. Facilities include showers, a grocery store, and a laundry room.

Food

Calgary may lack the cultural trappings that Alberta's capital, Edmonton, boasts, but it gives that city a run for its money in the restaurant department. Southwest of downtown, along 17th Avenue and 4th Street, a once-quieter part of the city has been transformed into a focal point for Calgary's restaurant scene, with cuisine to suit all tastes. Familiar North American fast-food restaurants line Macleod Trail south of the city center.

DOWNTOWN
Casual
All of the major high-rise buildings have plazas with inexpensive food courts and cafes—the perfect places for people watching. Local suits all have their own favorite haunts, but only two places really stand out to me as trying that little bit harder to be different and to please at the same time; both are owned by the same company. **Sunterra Village Marché** (Plus 15 Level, TransCanada Tower, 450 1st St. SW, 403/262-8240, Mon.–Fri. 6 A.M.–8 P.M.) is set up to represent a French streetscape, complete with a patisserie, carvery, salad counter, deli, wine bar, and juice joint. **Sunterra Marché** (Plus 15 Level, Bankers Hall, 855 2nd St. SW, 403/269-3610, Mon.–Fri. 6:30 A.M.–6:30 P.M., Sat. 9:30 A.M.–5:30 P.M.) has a much smaller selection, but the same high quality of gourmet-to-go lunches.

At the entrance to Prince's Island Park, **Eau Claire Market** has a large food court and several restaurants. In the food court, you'll find a great seafood outlet, a bakery, Asian-food places such as the Thai **Touch of Ginger** (403/234-8550), and an outlet of the local coffee chain **Good Earth Café** (403/237-8684). Outside the market's western entrance is ◖ **1886 Buffalo Café** (187 Barclay Pde. SW,

403/269-9255, Mon.–Fri. 6 A.M.–3 P.M., weekends 7 A.M.–3 P.M., breakfasts $9–14). Named for the year it was built, this restaurant oozes an authentic Old Calgary ambience. Inexpensive breakfasts attract the most interesting group of diners, but the place is busy all day.

Canadian
Thomsons (112 Stephen Ave. Walk, 403/537-4449, daily 6:30 A.M.–1:30 P.M. and 5–9:30 P.M., $20–36) is in a historic sandstone building cleverly integrated with the modern Hyatt Regency, but it's not aimed at the hotel crowd. First off, the buffet breakfast ($18) is as good as it gets, with omelets made to order and real maple syrup to douse your pancakes. The rest of the day, the menu is dominated by Canadian game and seafood. Maybe start with PEI mussels and bacon in traditional ale, then choose from something as Canadian as grilled arctic char or splurge on the Alberta beef tenderloin.

Walk north from Eau Claire Market to reach the ◖ **River Café** (Prince's Island Park, 403/261-7670, Mon.–Fri. 11 A.M.–11 P.M., Sat. and Sun. 11 A.M.–10 P.M., $24–49), a cozy, rustic dining room that will surprise you with some of Calgary's finest cooking. More of a restaurant than a café, it features extensive use of produce and ingredients sourced from across Canada. Standouts include buffalo, Alberta beef, and salmon dishes, with the latter often incorporating maple syrup. Lunch mains range $17–24 (including a delicious smoked trout flatbread) while weekend brunch ranges $11–19.

Had a bad experience dining in a revolving restaurant? Haven't we all. Hopefully your meal at the **Sky 360** (101 9th Ave. SW, 403/508-5822, daily 11–2 A.M. and 5 A.M.–10 P.M.,

$22–42) atop the Calgary Tower will be memorable for more than the view. A full rotation takes one hour. Expect healthy, modern cooking that uses lots of Canadian produce, with lunchtime sandwiches, such as maple-smoked chicken with apple chutney, for under $20. The

---

GOOD OL' ALBERTA BEEF

Although Alberta isn't renowned for its culinary delights, flavor-filled and tender Alberta beef is a provincial highlight. It's served at most Calgary restaurants, but only a few restaurants specialize in it. The following are my favorites.

Respected **Caesar's Steak House** (512 4th Ave. SW, 403/264-1222, Mon.-Fri. 11 A.M.-midnight, Sat. 4:30 P.M.-midnight, $28-47) has been around for over 30 years – a long time in the restaurant business. The elegant room has a Roman-style decor with dark wood, leather seating, and dim lighting – just what you expect from a steakhouse. Although the menu includes ribs and seafood, it's juicy prime cuts of Alberta beef that this place is known for.

Unlike Caesar's, **Saltlik** (101 8th Ave. SW, 403/537-1160, daily from 11 A.M. for lunch and dinner, $17-31) is anything but traditional. This stylish space filled with contemporary furniture packs in the lunchtime business crowd, but is also a good place for visitors to sample the best cuts of Alberta beef, which is flash-seared at super-high temperatures to seal in the juices.

The food at **Buzzard's Restaurant & Bar** (140 10th Ave., 403/264-6959, Mon.-Fri. 11 A.M.-11 P.M., Sat. 5-11 P.M., $21-26) doesn't come close to competing with the above two steakhouses, but that's not why I've included it. Buzzard's is fun. It's what everyone wants to think Calgary used to be like, but is about as authentic as downtown bankers wearing blue jeans for Stampede. Choices range from bison burgers to elk striploin, and it wouldn't be a complete meal at Buzzard's without sharing a platter of prairie oysters to start.

---

mushroom chowder is a good way to start, before moving on to mains such as a grilled pork chop that swims in a grainy mustard jus.

Seafood

Yes, Calgary is a long way from the ocean, but it nonetheless has a few excellent seafood restaurants. Across the railway tracks from downtown are two of the best: **Cannery Row** (317 10th Ave. SW, 403/269-8889) and, directly upstairs, **McQueens Upstairs** (403/269-4722). Cannery Row is a casual affair, with an open kitchen, an oyster bar, and the ambience of a San Francisco seafood restaurant. Dishes such as grilled swordfish, jambalaya, and blackened snapper are mostly under $20. The menu at McQueens Upstairs is more sophisticated and varied. Dinner entrées start at $21 and rise to over $40 for fresh lobster. Both restaurants are open Monday–Friday for lunch and daily for dinner.

Within the Hyatt Regency building, the sophisticated ambience of **Catch** (100 Stephen Ave. Walk, 403/206-0000, Mon.–Fri. 11:30 A.M.–1:30 P.M., Mon.–Sat. 5:30–9:30 P.M., $34–50) is as big an attraction as the menu of seasonal seafood that is flown in daily from both of Canada's coasts. The main level is an oyster bar, where you can sample a variety of shucked oysters with an extensive choice of drinks, while more formal dining is upstairs in the main room.

Smokehouse

In a city that has traditionally loved its beef, it should be no surprise that a Southern-style smokehouse is popular. One block off Stephen Avenue Walk, ◖ **Palomino** (109 7th Ave. SW, 403/532-1911, Mon.–Sat. for lunch and dinner, $17–24) fits the bill. The biggest change to a building that once held a furniture shop is a massive smoker capable of holding 300 kilograms (750 pounds) of meat at any one time. Forget about that diet and tuck into pork ribs ($17–24), giant Alberta beef ribs ($23), a "Fat Ass Platter" for four ($65), and, as the menu suggests, buy a round of drinks for the kitchen ($20). House wine choices range from "Cheap" to "Decent" and there are drink specials most nights.

Asian

Chinatown, along 2nd and 3rd Avenues east of Centre Street, naturally has the best assortment of Chinese restaurants. **Hang Fung Restaurant** (119 3rd Ave. SE, 403/269-4646, daily for lunch and dinner, $7–13), tucked behind a Chinese grocery store of the same name, doesn't try to be anything it's not. Chinese locals come here for simple inexpensive meals, mostly under $10. Just as inexpensive is **Golden Inn Restaurant** (107 2nd Ave. SE, 403/269-2211, daily from 4 P.M., $9–16), which is popular with the local Chinese as well as with professionals, and late-shift workers appreciate its long hours (open until 4 A.M.). The menu features mostly Cantonese-style deep-fried food.

Yuzuki Japanese Restaurant (510 9th Ave. SW, 403/261-7701, weekdays for lunch, daily for dinner, $13–19) is a good downtown eatery where the most expensive lunch item is the assorted sushi for $16, which comes with miso soup. More upscale is **Sushi Hiro** (727 5th Ave. SW, 403/233-0605, Mon.–Fri. 11:30 A.M.–2 P.M., Mon.–Sat. 5–11 P.M., $12–21). If you sit at the oak-and-green-marble sushi counter, you'll be able to ask the chef what's best.

Tucked away across the railway tracks from downtown is **(** **Thai Sa-On** (351 10th Ave. SW, 403/264-3526, dinner nightly, $11–17), a small space that's big on the tastes of Thailand. The menu offers a great variety of red and green curries, but I tried the red snapper—medium spiced, baked, and served whole—and couldn't have been happier. The prices? For downtown dining, the food is ridiculously inexpensive, with a whole steamed fish with garlic-lime sauce costing just $16.

KENSINGTON

Across the Bow River from downtown lies the trendy suburb of Kensington and **Higher Ground** (1126 Kensington Rd. NW, 403/270-3780, Mon.–Fri. 7 A.M.–10 P.M., Sat 8 A.M.–midnight, Sun. 8 A.M.–11 P.M.), a specialty coffee shop with a few window-front tables and wireless Internet.

The casual, two-story **(** **Pulcinella** (1147 Kensington Crescent NW, 403/283-1166, Mon.–Sat. 11:30 A.M.–2:30 P.M. and 5–11 P.M., Sun. 4–10 P.M., $12–24) has the most traditional pizza you will find in Canada, right down to an oven constructed of stone imported from the slopes of Mount Vesuvius. Pizzas have perfectly formed crusts and chunky ingredients, many of which have been imported from the mother country.

Sultan's Tent (4 14th St., 403/244-2333, Mon.–Sat. 5–11 P.M., $18–28.50) features swinging lanterns, richly colored tapestries hanging from the walls, piped-in Arabic music, and, most important, delicious Moroccan delicacies. If you're hungry, try the Sultan's Feast ($51), a five-course dinner.

A few blocks toward the city, Kensington's busiest intersection offers a bunch of eateries, including another Italian restaurant, **Osteria de Medici** (201 10th St. NW, 403/283-5553, Mon.–Sat. 11 A.M.–11 P.M., Sun. 4–10 P.M., $17–31). Although still traditional, the atmosphere is more refined and the menu more adventurous than Pulcinella, but service is friendly and prices not as high as they could be.

UPTOWN 17TH AVENUE

The area immediately south of downtown offers a diverse choice of dining options. The major concentrations of restaurants are along 17th Avenue SW as well as south for a couple of blocks along 4th Street. For gourmet coffees, hot chocolate made with locally made Bernard Callebaut chocolate, and exotic teas, join the crowds at **Café Beano** (1613 9th St. SW, 403/229-1232, daily 7 A.M.–11 P.M.).

Breakfast

(**Nellie's Kitchen** (738 17th Avenue SW, 403/244-4616, Mon.–Fri. 7:30 A.M.–3:30 P.M., Sat.–Sun. 8:30 A.M.–3:30 P.M., breakfasts $8–11), in the heart of Calgary's trendiest dining strip, is a pleasant surprise. It's a small, outwardly low-key place with a big reputation (so much so that it's now one of five Nellie's restaurants in the city). Service is fast and efficient and, most importantly, the food's great. Breakfasts claim the spotlight—if you're hungry, don't bother with the menu, just order the Belly Buster.

The **Galaxy Diner** (1413 11th St. SW, 403/228-0001, Mon.–Fri. 7 A.M.–3 P.M., Sat.–Sun. 7 A.M.–4 P.M.) is an original 1950s diner where cooked breakfasts start at $7.50, including bottomless coffee and a second serving of hash browns.

Canadian

Typifying the modern wave of slow food is **C FARM** (1006 17th Ave. SW, 403/245-2276, daily 11:30 A.M.–2 P.M. and from 5 P.M., $9–21), where the emphasis is on local, seasonal ingredients prepared in simple and tasty ways. Many diners concentrate on the meats and cheeses listed on a large chalkboard hanging on the back wall before moving onto house specialties such as killer BLT salad. The room itself is appealing, with stools along the open kitchen allowing diners to watch their meals being prepared by the friendly kitchen staff.

Formerly a brewpub, **Wildwood Grill** (2417 4th St., 402/228-0100, daily for lunch and dinner, $18–36) has evolved into a respected restaurant serving up a wide selection of Canadian cuisine in a modern mountain setting. Think leek and sweet corn soup or bison carpaccio as starters and grilled medallions of elk loin with spiced chocolate sauce for a main. In the adjacent pub, bring back childhood memories with a meatloaf ($15) that substitutes veal for beef.

European

Few restaurants in the city are as popular as **C Chianti** (1438 17th Ave. SW, 403/229-1600, Mon.–Fri. for lunch, daily for dinner, $10–20). More than 20 well-prepared pasta dishes are featured on the menu, and all of the pasta is made daily on the premises. Among many specialties are an antipasto platter and *salmone cappesante,* baked salmon with scallops and mango in a creamy coconut and curry sauce. Most regular pasta entrées are less than $12. The restaurant is dark and noisy in typical

© ANDREW HEMPSTEAD

For fresh, innovative cooking, make reservations at FARM.

Italian style. The owner often sings with an accordionist on weekends.

La Chaumiere (139 17th Ave. SW, 403/228-5690, Mon.–Fri. 11:45 A.M.–2:30 P.M. and Mon.–Sat. from 5:45 P.M., dinner reservations required, $26–36.50) occupies an elaborate space east of the main restaurant strip. Generally regarded as one of North America's premier French restaurants, diners here enjoy combinations like lobster bisque and roasted rack of Alberta lamb. The formal service is meticulous.

Information and Services

Information Centers

Tourism Calgary (403/263-8510 or 800/661-1678, www.tourismcalgary.com) promotes the city to the world. The organization also operates two Visitor Information Centres. The one that greets visitors arriving by air is across from Carousel 4 at **Calgary International Airport** (403/735-1234, year-round, daily 6 A.M.–11 P.M.). The other is right downtown, at the base of the **Calgary Tower** (101 9th Ave. SW, 403/750-2362, daily in summer 8 A.M.–8 P.M., the rest of the year Mon.–Fri. 8:30 A.M.–4:30 P.M.).

Libraries

The Calgary Public Library Board's 18 branch libraries are scattered throughout the city. The largest is **W. R. Castell Central Library** (616 Macleod Trail SE, 403/260-2600, www.calgarypubliclibrary.com, Mon.–Thurs. 9 A.M.–8 P.M., Fri. 9 A.M.–5 P.M., Sat. 10 A.M.–5 P.M., Sun. noon–5 P.M.). Four floors of books, magazines, and newspapers from around the world are enough to keep most people busy on a rainy afternoon.

Post and Internet

The downtown post office is at 207 9th Avenue SW. All city libraries provide free Internet access, while all downtown hotels have either wireless or modem Internet access. Alternatively, head to **Hard Disk Cafe** (638 11th Ave. SW, 403/261-5686, daily 7 A.M.–7 P.M.) for some online surfing.

Banks

Calforex, in the Lancaster Building (304 8th Ave. SW, 403/290-0330), exchanges foreign currency and lets you wire international payments. Most major banks carry U.S. currency and can handle basic foreign-exchange transactions.

Photography

I've been trusting my photographic needs to **The Camera Store** (802 11th Ave. SW, 403/234-9935, Mon.–Fri. 8 A.M.–5:30 P.M., Sat. 9 A.M.–5 P.M.) for many years. They have knowledgeable service and sales divisions, with the latter up to speed on the latest digital and video technology.

Laundry

Handy self-service launderettes are **14th Street Coin Laundry** (1211 14th St. SW, 403/541-1636, daily 7 A.M.–11 P.M.), which has washers big enough to handle sleeping bags and blankets, and **Heritage Hill Coin Laundry** (156-8228 MacLeod Trail SE, 403/258-3946).

Emergency Services

For medical emergencies, call 911 or contact **Foothills Hospital** (1403 29th Ave. NW, 403/670-1110) or **Rockyview General Hospital** (7007 14th St. SW, 403/943-3000). Opened in late 2006 across 16th Avenue from Foothills Hospital, the **Alberta Children's Hospital** (2888 Shaganappi Trail NW, 403/955-7211) is difficult to miss with its colorfully modern exterior. For the **Calgary Police,** call 911 in an emergency or 403/266-1234 for non-urgent matters.

Getting There and Around

GETTING THERE
Air
Calgary International Airport (airport code YYC; www.calgaryairport.com) is within the city limits northeast of downtown. It is served by more than a dozen scheduled airlines and used by seven million passengers each year (Canada's fourth-busiest airport). Arrivals is on the lower level, where passengers are greeted by White Hat volunteers who are dressed in traditional Western attire and answer visitors' questions about the airport, transportation, and the city. Across from the baggage carousels is an information desk and a bank of interactive computer terminals linked to hotels and other tourist services. The desks for all major rental-car outlets are across the road.

A cab to downtown runs approximately $40, or take the **Allied Airport Shuttle** (403/299-9555, www.airportshuttlecalgary.com) to major downtown hotels for adult $15, child $10 one-way. This service runs every 30 minutes daily 8 A.M.–midnight.

For details of airlines flying into Calgary, click through the links on the airport website.

Bus
The **Greyhound** bus depot (850 16th St. SW, 403/265-9111 or 800/661-8747, www.greyhound.ca) is two blocks away from the C-train stop ($2 into town), or you can cross the overhead pedestrian bridge at the terminal's southern entrance and catch a transit bus. A cab from the bus depot to downtown runs $12, to HI–Calgary City Centre $15. Greyhound buses connect Calgary daily with Edmonton (3.5 hours), Banff (two hours), Vancouver (15 hours), and all other points within the province.

From their offices near the Calgary Tower, **Red Arrow** (205 9th Ave. SE, 403/531-0350, www.redarrow.ca) shuttles passengers between Calgary and downtown Edmonton, with some services continuing to Fort McMurray in northern Alberta.

GETTING AROUND
Like major cities around the world, locals complain about the road system, but in reality, driving is relatively uncomplicated, especially as new sections of the long-awaited ring road are completed.

Calgary Transit
Calgary Transit (403/262-1000, www.calgarytransit.com) goes just about everywhere in town by combining light-rail lines with extensive bus routes. **C-trains** run along the two rail lines totaling 40 kilometers (25 mi) of track and 36 stations. Both converge on 7th Avenue, running parallel for the entire distance through downtown. One-way bus and rail tickets are adult $2.50, child $1.75—deposit the exact change in the box beside the driver and request a transfer (valid for 90 minutes). A day pass, which is valid for unlimited bus and rail travel, is adult $7.50, child $5.25. The best place for information and schedules is the **Calgary Transit Customer Service Centre** (244 7th Ave. SW, Mon.–Fri. 10 A.M.–5 P.M.).

All C-trains and stations are wheelchair accessible. Low-floor buses are employed on many bus routes; call ahead for a schedule. **Calgary Handi-bus** (403/537-7770, www.calgaryhandibus.com) provides wheelchair-accessible transportation throughout the city.

Taxi
The flag charge for a cab in Calgary is $3.40, and it's around $1.40 for every kilometer. Taxi companies include **Advance** (403/777-1111), **Associated Cabs** (403/299-1111), **Checker/Yellow Cabs** (403/299-9999), and **Mayfair** (403/255-6555).

Car Rental
If you're planning on starting your Alberta travels from Calgary and need a rental car, make reservations as far in advance as possible to secure the best rates. Rentals beginning from the airport incur additional charges, so

consider renting from downtown or one of the many hotels that have representatives based in their lobbies.

Rental agencies and their local numbers include: **Avis** (403/269-6166), **Budget** (403/226-1550), **Discount** (403/299-1224), **Economy** (403/291-1640), **Enterprise** (403/263-1273), **Hertz** (403/221-1676), **National** (403/221-1690), **Rent-a-Wreck** (403/287-9703), and **Thrifty** (403/262-4400).

Dinosaur Valley

The most worthwhile non-mountain day trip from Calgary is to Dinosaur Valley, a 90-minute drive from city limits. Centered on the Red Deer River, a 120-kilometer (75-mile) stretch of the river valley is home to some of the world's richest dinosaur fossil beds. Hundreds of specimens from the Cretaceous period have been unearthed, with one spot, Dinosaur Provincial Park, the mother lode for paleontologists. This UNESCO World Heritage Site includes a "graveyard" of more than 300 dinosaurs of 35 species, many of which have been found nowhere else in the world. As a comparison, Utah's Dinosaur National Monument has yielded just 12 species. The valley has more than just dinosaur skeletons, though; paleontologists have unearthed skin impressions, eggshells, dung, and footprints, as well as fossilized insects, fish, amphibians, crocodiles, pterodactyls, and reptiles. And the valley's landforms are as enthralling as the prehistoric artifacts they entomb—spectacular badland formations make for a sight not easily forgotten.

DRUMHELLER

The small city of Drumheller (population 8,000) is set in a spectacular lunar-like landscape in the Red Deer River Valley 138 kilometers (86 miles) northeast of Calgary. Paleontologists from around the globe come to

Drumheller is renowned for its dinosaur-related attractions.

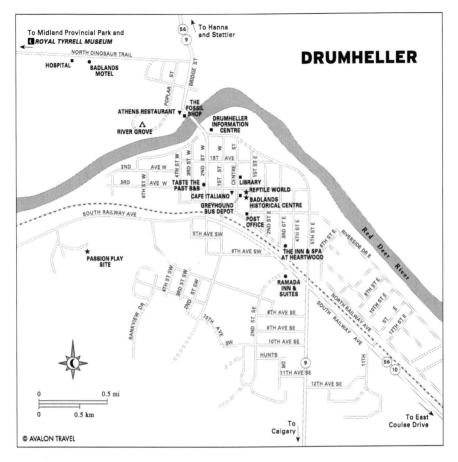

Drumheller and its environs to learn more about the prehistoric animals that roamed the earth millions of years ago. For tourists, the Royal Tyrrell Museum is definitely the highlight of a visit to Drumheller, but there are many other diversions along the valley. Downtown itself is a little rough around the edges, but has been bought to life in recent years with the addition of dinosaur sculptures and murals.

◖ Royal Tyrrell Museum

So many of the world's great museums are simply showcases for natural history, yet nestled in the badlands six kilometers (3.7 mi) northwest

of Drumheller, the Royal Tyrrell Museum (North Dinosaur Trail, 403/823-7707 or 888/440-4240, www.tyrrellmuseum.com, mid-May–Aug. daily 9 A.M.–9 P.M., the rest of the year Tues.–Sun. 10 A.M.–5 P.M., adult $10, senior $8, youth $6, under six free), the world's largest museum devoted entirely to paleontology, is a lot more. It integrates display areas with fieldwork done literally on the doorstep (it lies close by that first "official" discovery), with specimens transported to the museum for research and cataloging. Even for those visitors with little or no interest in dinosaurs, it's easy to spend half a day in the massive complex. The

THE GREAT DINOSAUR RUSH

For generations, natives had regarded the ancient bones that were always common in the valley as belonging to giant buffalo. During early geographical surveys of southern Alberta by George Mercer Dawson, the first official dinosaur discovery was recorded. In 1884, one of Dawson's assistants, Joseph Burr Tyrrell, collected and sent specimen bones to Ottawa for scientific investigation. Their identification initiated the first real dinosaur rush. For the first century of digging, all of the dinosaur bones uncovered were transported to museums around the world for further study. Just more than 100 years after Tyrrell's discovery, a magnificent museum bearing his name opened in the valley. The idea of the museum was promoted by dinosaur hunter Dr. Phil Currie, and since its opening, the dinosaurs have stayed and the tourists have come.

museum holds more than 80,000 specimens, including 50 full-size dinosaur skeletons—the world's largest such display.

The adventure starts as soon as you enter the facility, with a group of life-sized Albertosaurus dinosaurs in a Cretaceous setting to welcome you. Beyond the lobby is a massive, slowly-revolving model of the earth set against a starry night—a perfect introduction to this planet's place in the universe. Beyond the globe, a "timeline" of exhibits covers 3.8 billion years of life on this planet, beginning with early life forms and the development of Charles Darwin's theory of evolution. Before the age of the dinosaurs, the Precambrian and Paleozoic eras saw life on Earth develop at an amazing rate. These periods are cataloged through numerous displays, such as the one of British Columbia's Burgess Shale, where circumstances allowed the fossilization of a community of soft-bodied marine creatures 530 million years ago. But the museum's showpiece is Dinosaur Hall, a vast open area where reconstructed skeletons

and full-size replicas of dinosaurs are backed by realistic dioramas of their habitat. Another feature is the two-story paleoconservatory, featuring more than 100 species of plants, many of which flourished during the period when dinosaurs roamed the earth. Nearing the end of the tour, the various theories for the cause of the dinosaurs' extinction approximately 64 million years ago are presented. The coming of the ice ages is described in detail, and humanity's appearance on Earth is put into perspective.

The museum is also a major research center; a large window into the main preparation laboratory allows you to view the delicate work of technicians as they clear the rock away from newly unearthed bones.

Other Dinosaur Distractions

Start your downtown Drumheller touring by making your way to the visitor center, at the north end of 2nd Street W and signposted along all approaches. It's impossible to miss—out front is the world's largest dinosaur (403/823-8100, July–Aug. daily 9 A.M.–9 P.M., Sept.–June daily 10 A.M.–5:30 P.M., adult $2, children under five free). An actual *Tyrannosaurus rex* would have been intimidating enough towering over its fellow creatures millions of years ago. But this one is even bigger—at 26 meters (85 feet) high, it is four times as big as the real thing. A flight of stairs leads up to a viewpoint in its open mouth. Also downtown, the **Badlands Historical Centre** (335 1st St. E, 403/823-2593, May–Sept. daily 10 A.M.–6 P.M., adult $5) is a small museum with an interesting display of privately owned and donated prehistoric pieces, most of which have been collected from the Red Deer River Valley.

Along North Dinosaur Trail is **Fossil World** (1381 North Dinosaur Trail, 403/823-4333, summer daily 9:30 A.M.–7 P.M., the rest of the year daily 10 A.M.–5 P.M.) is a modern indoor attraction anchored by a life-size animated Tyrannosaurus rex. The seven-meter-long (21-foot) creature towers above the display room, with eyes that blink, a chest that contracts, and even a wagging tail. A number of interesting fossils are on display and for kids, there's also a

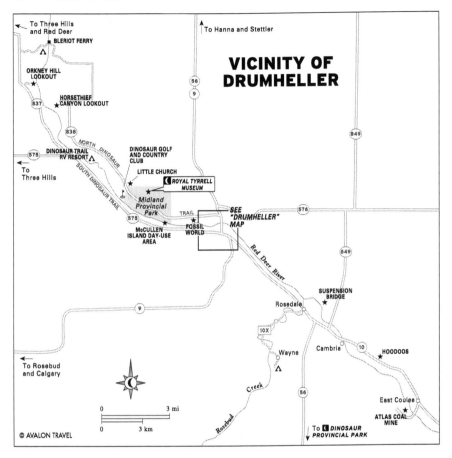

VICINITY OF DRUMHELLER

To Three Hills and Red Deer
To Hanna and Stettler
BLERIOT FERRY
ORKNEY HILL LOOKOUT
HORSETHIEF CANYON LOOKOUT
837
838
NORTH DINOSAUR
575
DINOSAUR TRAIL RV RESORT
To Three Hills
DINOSAUR GOLF AND COUNTRY CLUB
LITTLE CHURCH
ROYAL TYRRELL MUSEUM
SOUTH DINOSAUR TRAIL
Midland Provincial Park
575
McCULLEN ISLAND DAY-USE AREA
TRAIL
FOSSIL WORLD
SEE "DRUMHELLER" MAP
576
849
Red Deer River
849
SUSPENSION BRIDGE
9
Rosedale
10X
Wayne
Cambria
10
HOODOOS
To Rosebud and Calgary
Creek
56
East Coulee
ATLAS COAL MINE
0   3 mi
0   3 km
© AVALON TRAVEL
Rosebud
To DINOSAUR PROVINCIAL PARK

climbing wall, dinosaur-themed play area, and the chance to dig for (and keep) a fossil. General admission for everyone aged four or more is $5, or pay $22 for admission and all activities.

Scenic Drives

The **Dinosaur Trail** is a 56-kilometer (35-mile) circular route to the west of Drumheller. From downtown, head out toward the museum, passing **Midland Provincial Park,** where buildings from the coal mining era remain and an island in the Red Deer River is home to a day-use area shaded by willows and cottonwoods. Beyond the Royal Tyrrell Museum, the road climbs steeply

out of the valley onto the prairie benchland. Take the first access road on the left—it doubles back to **Horsethief Canyon Lookout,** where you can catch spectacular views of the badlands and the multicolored walls of the canyons. Slip, slide, or somersault down the embankment here into the mysterious lunar-like landscape, and it's easy to imagine why early explorers were so intrigued by the valley and how easy it was for thieves to hide stolen horses along the coulees in the early 1900s. The halfway point of the trail is the crossing of the Red Deer River on the eight-vehicle **Bleriot Ferry** (8 a.m.–10:40 p.m. Apr.–Nov.), one of the few remaining cable ferries in Alberta. The road continues along the top of the valley to **Orkney Hill Lookout** for more panoramic views across the badlands and the lush valley floor.

The 25-kilometer (15.5-mile) **East Coulee Drive,** southeast from Drumheller, passes three historic coal-mining communities in an area dotted with mine shafts and abandoned buildings. The first town along this route is **Rosedale,** from where a suspension bridge leads across the river to an abandoned mine site. A worthwhile detour from Rosedale is to **Wayne,** an almost–ghost town tucked up a valley alongside Rosebud Creek. It is nine kilometers (5.6 miles) south along Highway 10X, which crosses the creek 11 times. In its heyday early in the 20th century, Wayne had 1,500 residents, most of whom worked in the Rosedeer Mine. By the time the mine closed in 1962, the population had dipped to 250 and then to as low as 15 in the early 1990s, but now the population stands at approximately 30. Many old buildings remain, making it a popular setting for film crews. The oldest operating business in the sleepy hamlet is the 1913 **Rosedeer Hotel** (403/823-9189) and its **Last Chance Saloon,** where the walls are lined with memorabilia from the town's glory days. It opens daily at noon, just in time for a lunchtime buffalo burger. The hotel's back porch overlooking the creek is a great place to sip on a beer and wallow in nostalgia. From Rosedale, Highway 10 continues southeast, passing **hoodoos** to the left. These strangely shaped rock formations along the river valley have been carved by eons of wind and rain. The harder rock on top is more resistant to erosion than the rock beneath it, resulting in the odd, mushroom-shaped pillars. At East Coulee, the **Atlas Coal Mine** (403/823-2220, May–June daily 9:30 A.M.–5:30 P.M., July–Aug. daily 9:30 A.M.–8:30 P.M., Sept.–mid-Oct. daily 10 A.M.–5 P.M., $7, tours $9–12 include admission) protects Canada's only remaining wooden ore-sorting tipple.

Performing Arts

At the hamlet of **Rosebud,** 35 kilometers (22 miles) southwest of Drumheller, students in residence showcase their performance skills at the **Rosebud Theatre** (403/677-2001 or 800/267-7553, www.rosebudtheatre.com). The fun actually starts across the road from the theater in the restored Mercantile Building, where the actors and actresses serve up a buffet meal. Then everyone heads over to the 220-seat theater for a lively production, always lighthearted and often with a rural theme. Check the website for a schedule.

The **Canadian Badlands Passion Play** (17th Street, 403/823-2001, adult $32, child $15) is a theatrical production of the life of Jesus Christ. The three-hour production is an ambitious affair, with a cast of hundreds in a natural outdoor amphitheater with bench seating for 2,500 set among the badlands. It takes place six times through the month of July.

Accommodations

Despite its popularity as a tourist attraction, Drumheller has a limited number of accommodations. Therefore, unless you're planning a day trip from Calgary, make reservations in advance.

Right on the main thoroughfare through downtown, **Taste the Past B&B** (281 2nd St. W, 403/823-5889, $95 s, $115 d) occupies the 100-year-old home of a coal baron. Guests choose between three simple rooms, but no one chooses to miss the full-cooked breakfast served in the sunny dining room. Period furnishings decorate public areas, including the living room, which is laid out around a fireplace. Outside, the well-tended garden is dotted with fossils.

Within walking distance of downtown is █ **The Inn & Spa at Heartwood** (320 Railway Ave. East, 403/823-6495 or 888/823-6495, www.innsatheartwood.com, $149–309 s or d), a classic country inn that looks a little out of place surrounded by older homes. You can splurge on the Main Turret room with a carriage bed, a fireplace, a jetted tub, and separate sitting area. Or choose one of eight other rooms, all with a cozy Victorian feel thanks to antiques and plush duvets. All rooms have en suites, but only some have televisions and phones. Rates include breakfast.

Ramada Inn & Suites (680 2nd St., 403/823-2028 or 800/272-6232, $149–249 s or d) is at Drumheller's busiest intersection. The 74 rooms are each equipped with a small fridge and a microwave. Rates include a light breakfast and use of the indoor pool, waterslide, fitness room, and hot tub.

Camping

Plenty of choices here, but reservations should still be made as far in advance as possible.

A personal favorite is **Ⓒ Dinosaur Trail RV Resort** (11 km/7 mi along North Dinosaur Trail, 403/823-9333, www.holidaytrailsresorts.com, May–Sept., $31–48), an oasis of green between the river and the badlands five kilometers (3.1 mi) beyond the Tyrrell Museum. Activities include river floats, fishing, cooling off in the outdoor pool, or exploring the adjacent badlands on foot. Other facilities include horseshoe pits, a playground, a grocery store, and a laundry.

Back toward Drumheller, **River Grove Campground** (25 Poplar St., 403/823-6655, May–Sept., tent sites $25, hookups $29–36) is in a well-treed spot beside the Red Deer River and also offers welcome relief from the heat of the badlands. Serviced sites are semiprivate; tenters have more options and are able to disappear among the trees. The campground offers a nice stretch of sandy beach (by Albertan standards), mini-golf, and an arcade; and town is just a short stroll away.

At the end of the Dinosaur Trail is **Bleriot Ferry Provincial Recreation Area** ($15) with 28 sites, plenty of free firewood, a kitchen shelter, and a small beach on the river.

Food

Like the accommodation scene, finding a restaurant in Drumheller is easy enough; finding a place you'll leave saying "that was a good meal" is a different matter. The cafeteria at the **Royal Tyrell Museum** (North Dinosaur Trail, 403/823-7707, mid-May–Aug. daily 9 A.M.–6 P.M., the rest of the year Tues.–Sun. 10 A.M.–3:30 P.M.) is one of the better spots to enjoy lunch, especially sitting on the patio on a sunny day.

At the Badlands Motel, out toward the museum, **Whif's Flapjack House** (801 N.

Dinosaur Trail, 403/823-7595, 6 A.M.–2 P.M.) serves up a continuous flow of pancakes ($5–8) from when the doors first open each morning.

Downtown, **Café Italiano** (35 3rd Ave. W, 403/823-4443, Mon.–Fri. 7 A.M.–5 P.M., Sat. 9 A.M.–5 P.M., lunches $5–9) pours the best coffee in town. Also on offer are paninis, salads, and homemade desserts.

Athens Restaurant (71 Bridge St. N, 403/823-9400, Mon.–Sat. 4–9 P.M., $16–25) has been around for decades. Although the service is not overly friendly the food is decent. The house specialty is *kleftiko* (spring lamb baked with herbs and spices); have it with the Greek salad for the full effect.

Information and Services

Drumheller Information Centre is in the local chamber of commerce building beside the Red Deer River at the corner of Riverside Drive and 2nd Street W (403/823-8100 or 866/823-3100, www.traveldrumheller.com, daily 9 A.M.–6 P.M., until 9 P.M. Fri. and Sat. in summer). You can't miss it—look for the seven-story *Tyrannosaurus rex* in front.

Drumheller Public Library (224 Centre Street, 403/823-5382, Tues.–Thurs. 11 A.M.–8 P.M., Fri. and Sat. 11 A.M.–5 P.M., Sun. 1–5 P.M.) has public Internet access.

The **post office** is at 96 Railway Avenue E. You can wash your dusty clothes at the **launderette** in the Esso gas station on Highway 9 on the south side of town. It's open until 8 P.M. **Drumheller Hospital** is across the river from downtown at 351 9th St. NW (403/823-6500).

Ⓒ DINOSAUR PROVINCIAL PARK

Now that you've been through the Royal Tyrrell Museum, you'll want to get out in the field and explore the area where many of the dinosaurs have been unearthed. This region is protected by 7,330-hectare (18,000-acre) Dinosaur Provincial Park, 120 kilometers (75 miles) downstream of Drumheller. It's possible to get there by road from Drumheller—east on

Highway 570 then south on Highway 36—but, from Calgary, the direct route is 200 kilometers (125 miles) east along Highway 1.

Thirty-five species of dinosaurs—from every known family of the Cretaceous period—have been unearthed here, along with the skeletal remains of crocodiles, turtles, fish, lizards, frogs, and flying reptiles. Not only is the diversity of specimens great, but so is the sheer volume; more than 300 museum-quality specimens have been removed and are exhibited in museums around the world. Originally established in 1955 to protect the fossil bone beds, the park's environment is extremely complex and is unique within the surrounding prairie ecosystem. Stands of cottonwoods, a variety of animal life, and, most important, the extensive bone beds, were instrumental in UNESCO's designation of the park as a World Heritage Site in 1979. The Royal Tyrrell Museum operates a field station in the park, where many of the bones are cataloged and stored.

Fieldwork in the Park

Each summer, paleontologists from around the world converge on the park for an intense period of digging that starts in late June and lasts for approximately 10 weeks. The earliest dinosaur hunters simply excavated whole or partial skeletons for museum display. Although the basic excavation methods haven't changed, the types of excavation have. "Bonebeds" of up to one hectare are painstakingly excavated over multiple summers. Access to much of the park is restricted in order to protect the fossil beds. Digging takes place within the restricted areas. Work is often continued from the previous season, or commences on new sites, but

DINOSAURS OF ALBERTA

Dinosaur bones found in the Red Deer River Valley play an important role in the understanding of our prehistoric past. The bones date from the late Cretaceous period, around 70 million years ago, when the area was a low-lying subtropical forest at the mouth of a river flowing into the ocean – and dinosaurs flourished.

Around this time, great quantities of silt and mud were flushed downriver, building up a delta at the edge of the sea. In time, this delta hardened, and the countless layers formed sedimentary rock, trapping the remains of fallen dinosaurs. As the Red Deer River curves through central Alberta, it cuts deeply into the ancient river delta, exposing the layers of sedimentary rock and revealing the once-buried fossil treasures.

The bones of 35 dinosaur species – around 10 percent of all those currently known – have been discovered in Alberta. Like today's living creatures, they are classified in orders, families, and species. Of the two orders of dinosaurs, both have been found in the Red Deer River Valley. The bird-hipped dinosaurs (order Ornithischia) were herbivores, while the lizard-

hipped dinosaurs (order Saurischia) were omnivores and carnivores.

Apart from their sheer bulk, many herbivores lacked any real defenses. Others developed their own protection; the chasmosaurus had a bony frill around its neck, the pachycephalosaurus had a 25-centimeter-thick (10-inch-thick) dome-shaped skull cap fringed with spikes, and the ankylosaurus was an armored dinosaur whose back was covered in spiked plates.

Among the most common herbivores that have been found in the valley are members of the family of duck-billed hadrosaurs. Fossilized eggs of one hadrosaur, the hypacrosaurus, were unearthed still encasing intact embryos. Another common herbivore in the valley was a member of the horned ceratops family; more than 300 specimens of the centrosaurus have been discovered in one "graveyard."

Of the lizard-hipped dinosaurs, the tyrannosaurs were most feared by herbivores. The 15-meter (49-foot) *Tyrannosaurus rex* is most famous among *Homo sapiens*, but the smaller albertosaurus, a remarkably agile carnivore weighing many tons, was the most common tyrannosaur found in the valley.

there's never a lack of bones. New finds are often discovered with little digging, having been exposed by wind and rain since the previous season.

Excavating the bones is an extremely tedious procedure; therefore, only a few sites are worked on at a time, with preference given to particularly important finds such as a new species. Getting the bones out of the ground is only the beginning of a long process that culminates with their scientific analysis and display by experts at museums around the world.

Visitors Center

Your first stop should be the Dinosaur Park Visitor Centre (403/378-4342, Apr.–mid-May daily 9 A.M.–4 P.M., mid-May–Aug. daily 8:30 A.M.–7 P.M., Sept. 9 A.M.–4:30 P.M., the rest of the year weekdays 9 A.M.–4 P.M., adult $3, senior $2.50, child $2), which is a field station associated with the Royal Tyrrell Museum. It offers many interesting displays that provide an overview of the park, its natural history, and the dinosaurs contained within. Complete dinosaur skeletons, a reconstructed 1914 paleontologist field camp, and a dinosaur documentary are highlights.

Interpretive Tours

To make the most of your time in the park, you will want to join one of the park's daily tours. Not only do the guides provide an insight into the area, but some of the tours concentrate on the natural preserve where unguided public access is not allowed. The tours are *very* popular, and this is reflected in the procedure for purchasing tickets. Advance tickets (adult $8, child $4) go on sale May 1 and must be picked up 30 minutes before the departure time. To reserve a seat, click through the Reservations link at www.tpr.alberta.ca/parks/dinosaur or call 403/378-4344. A small percentage of places on each tour are sold the day of as Rush tickets (adult $6.50, child $4.50); be at the visitor center when it opens at 8:30 A.M. to ensure that you get a ticket. Finally, if seats become available through no-shows, you may be able to snag a seat at the last minute. An overview

of the tours follows, or check www.tpr.alberta.ca/parks/dinosaur for a schedule.

The **Badlands Bus Tour** takes you on a two-hour ride around the public loop road with an interpretive guide who will point out the park's landforms and talk about its prehistoric inhabitants. The **Centrosaurus Bone Bed Hike** takes visitors on a 2.5-hour guided hike into a restricted area where more than 300 centrosaurus skeletons have been identified. The **Camel's End Coulee Hike** is an easy 2.5-kilometer (1.5-mi) guided walk to discover the unique flora and fauna of the badlands. Best suited for families with younger children is the **Fossil Safari Hike** to a dig site. Finally, the **Lab Talk** is a 40-minute behind-the-scenes look at the visitor center. This is the only tour that doesn't require reservations; adult $4, child $2.

Documentaries are shown at the visitor center in the evenings, and special events are often staged somewhere in the park. The entire interpretive program operates June–August, with certain tours offered in late May and September.

Exploring the Park on Your Own

Much of the park is protected as a Natural Preserve and is off-limits to unguided visitors. The Natural Preserve protects the bone beds and the valley's fragile environment. It also keeps visitors from becoming disoriented in the uniform landscape and ending up spending the night among the bobcats and rattlesnakes. The area is well marked and should not be entered except on a guided tour. One other important rule: *Surface-collecting and digging for bones anywhere within the park is prohibited.*

You may explore the area bounded by the public loop road and take three short interpretive trails on your own. The **loop road** passes through part of the area where bones were removed during the Great Canadian Dinosaur Rush. By staying within its limits, hikers are prevented from becoming lost, although the classic badlands terrain is still littered with fragments of bones, and the area is large enough to make you feel "lost in time." It's a fantastic place to explore. Of special interest are two dinosaur dig sites excavated earlier this century, one of which contains a still-intact skeleton of a duck-billed hadrosaur.

The **Badlands Trail** is a 1.3-kilometer (0.8-mile) loop that starts just east of the campground and passes into the restricted area. The **Coulee Viewpoint Trail,** which begins behind the Field Station, climbs steadily for 500 meters (1,650 feet) to a high ridge above Little Sandhill Creek. This one-kilometer (0.6-mile) trail takes 20 minutes. It's easy to ignore the nearby floodplains, but the large stands of cottonwoods you'll see were a contributing factor to the park being designated as a UNESCO World Heritage Site. The **Cottonwood Flats Trail** starts 1.4 kilometers (0.9 miles) along the loop road, leading through the trees and into old river channels that lend themselves to good bird-watching. Allow 30 minutes round-trip.

Practicalities

The park's campground is nestled below the badlands beside Little Sandhill Creek. It has 128 sites on 2 loops, pit toilets, a kitchen shelter, and a few powered sites. Unserviced sites cost $20, powered sites $26, and a bundle of firewood is $7. In summer, the campground fills up by early afternoon, so plan ahead by reserving a site (403/378-3700, www.reserve.albertaparks.ca). The only commercial facility within the park is the **Dinosaur Service Centre** (403/378-3777, late May–Aug. daily 10 A.M.–6 P.M.), where you can purchase hot snacks and cold drinks. Within the center are laundry facilities and coin showers, both of which are open 24 hours. No groceries are available in the park.

For information, contact Dinosaur Provincial Park at 403/378-4342, www.tpr.alberta.ca/parks/dinosaur.

BROOKS

The closest mid-sized town to Dinosaur Provincial Park is Brooks (pop. 14,000), 160 kilometers (100 mi) east of Calgary along the TransCanada Highway. Brooks is home to Canada's largest meatpacking plant. The facility employs around 2,500 people, most of them immigrants from places like Sudan and Kenya. This gives Brooks an interesting small-town ethnic diversity unlike anywhere else in Canada.

The 3.2-kilometer-long (two-mile) **Brooks Aqueduct,** seven kilometers (4.3 miles) southeast of town, was completed in 1914 to carry water across a shallow valley to dry prairie on the other side, opening up a massive chunk of otherwise unproductive land to farming. Although now replaced by an earth-filled canal, the impressive structure has been preserved as a National Historic Site and now serves as a monument to those who developed the region.

Also south of town is **Kinbrook Island Provincial Park,** linked to the mainland by a causeway but best known for recreational activities on adjacent Lake Newell, Canada's largest man-made body of water. For visitors, it's swimming, fishing, and boating that draws the summertime crowds. The campground (403/362-2962, unserviced sites $20, powered sites $26) has showers, laundry, firewood sales, and picnic shelters.

West of Calgary

Between the snowcapped peaks of Kananaskis Country and the arid grassland of southern Alberta lies some of North America's best ranching country. From Cochrane in the north, throughout the ranching and farming communities of Okotoks and High River, to the Porcupine Hills northwest of Fort Macleod, these low, rolling hills have been home to many

of western Canada's cowboy heroes and the setting for movies such as the Jackie Chan hit *Shanghai Noon;* the Oscar-winning *Unforgiven,* starring Clint Eastwood; *Legends of the Fall,* starring Brad Pitt; the Kevin Costner western *Open Range;* and most recently the Brad Pitt–driven *The Assassination of Jesse James by the Coward Robert Ford.* Highway 2 follows the eastern flanks of these foothills south from Calgary. Other roads crisscross the region and lead to communities that are rich in heritage, many of which have recently been discovered by artisans and craftspeople who now call them home.

If you have ever dreamed of being a cowboy for a day or a week, this is the place to do it. The area also offers enough museums, teahouses, antique emporiums, and events to keep even the most saddle-sore city slicker busy all summer.

COCHRANE

The foundation of Alberta's cattle industry was laid down here in the 20th century, when Senator Matthew Cochrane established the first of the big leasehold ranches in the province. Today's town of Cochrane, 38 kilometers (24 miles) northwest of downtown Calgary along Highway 1A, has seen its population increase by over 10 percent annually since the mid 1990s, now sitting at over 15,000. Although ranching is still important to the local economy, Cochrane is growing as a "bedroom" suburb of Calgary. The business district, in the older section of town between Highway 1A and the rail line, is a delightful pocket of false-fronted buildings holding cafés, restaurants, and specialty shops.

Sights and Recreation

To prevent the lawlessness that existed across the U.S. West from extending into Canada, the government began granting huge grazing leases across the prairies. One of the original takers was Matthew Cochrane, who established the first real ranch west of Calgary, bringing herds of cattle from Montana to his 76,500-hectare (189,000-acre) holding in 1881. After two harsh winters, he moved his herds south again. A small piece of Cochrane's land holding is now preserved as **Cochrane Ranche Provincial Historic Site.** Almost completely surrounded by development, the 61-hectare (150-acre) site straddles Big Hill Creek one kilometer (0.6 miles) west of downtown along Highway 1A. A short trail leads up to a bluff and Malcolm MacKenzie's *Men of Vision* statue of a rider and his horse looking over the

foothills. An old log cabin by the parking lot is used as an interpretive center (403/932-1193, 9 A.M.–5 P.M. mid-May–Sept.) and picnic tables dot the grounds.

Immerse yourself in the Western lifestyle at **Griffin Valley Ranch** (403/932-7433), one of the few places in Alberta that allows unguided horseback riding. Trails lead through this historic 1,800-hectare (4,500-acre) ranch along creeks, through wooded areas and open meadows, and to high viewpoints where the panorama extends west to the Canadian Rockies. Horse rentals are similarly priced to trail riding (one hour $35, two hours $55, three hours $75); the catch is that at least one member of your party must be a "member" of the ranch (simply sign a waiver and pay the $50 annual fee). To get to the ranch, follow Highway 1A west from Cochrane for 18 kilometers (11 miles), take Highway 40 north, then follow the signs.

Accommodations and Food

You'll find Western-style on a budget at the **Rocky View Hotel** (1st St. and 2nd Ave. W, 403/932-2442, www.rockyviewhotel.com, $55–80 s or d). Rooms are very basic, with shared bathroom facilities and no phones. **Bow River Inn** (Hwy. 22, south of Hwy. 1A, 403/932-7900 or 866/663-3209, www.bowriverinn.com, $89 s or d, kitchenette $129) is a pleasant, reasonably priced motel with a choice of family restaurants within walking distance.

Two kilometers (1.2 miles) south of downtown is **Bow RiversEdge Campground** (900 Griffin Rd., 403/932-4675, www.bowriversedge.com, mid-Apr.–mid-Oct., $35–40), which has a wealth of modern facilities that include Wi-Fi, a playground, and a laundry.

 Cochrane Coffee Traders (114 2nd Ave., 403/932-4395, daily from 7:30 A.M.) is as good as any place to start the day, especially if you snag one of the outdoor tables. Choose from a wide range of specialty coffees and sweet treats, as well as a healthy selection of sandwiches. Back on 1st Street is the two-story wooden-fronted **Rocky View Hotel** (304 1st St. W, 403/932-2442) which houses the **Canyon Rose Restaurant,** a popular all-day dining spot, and the **Stageline Saloon.** Of the many eateries lining Cochrane's downtown 1st Street, the most popular on a hot summer's afternoon is **Mackay's** (403/932-2455), an ice-cream parlor dating to 1948. A blackboard displays up to 50 flavors, but I'm told the favorites are still vanilla, chocolate, and strawberry.

BRAGG CREEK

Bragg Creek is a quiet hamlet nestled in the foothills of the Canadian Rockies, 34 kilometers (21 miles) south of Cochrane. The ideal location and quiet lifestyle have attracted artists and artisans—the town claims to have more painters, potters, sculptors, and weavers than any similarly sized town in Alberta.

Sights

Arriving along Highway 22 from either the north or south, you'll be greeted upon arrival in Bragg Creek by a slightly confusing four-way stop intersection with a treed triangle of land in the middle. Take the option along the north (right) side of the distinctive polished-log Bragg Creek Trading Post II to access the main shopping center, a Western-themed collection of basic town services interspersed with craft shops and cafés. White Avenue, also known as **Heritage Mile** and originally the main commercial strip, has more of the same and leads through an appealing residential area. This road continues southwest to 122-hectare (300-acre) **Bragg Creek Provincial Park,** a day-use area alongside the Elbow River. With a basket of goodies from one of Bragg Creek's many food outlets, leave the main parking lot behind to enjoy a picnic lunch at one of the many riverside picnic tables.

Accommodations and Food

Although lacking motels and campgrounds, Bragg Creek is a popular overnight escape for folks from Calgary. Best of a bunch of bed-and-breakfasts is **High Country House** (call for directions, 403/949-0093, www.high-countryhouse.com, $148–185 s or d), a large, modern house nestled among stands of trees within walking distance of both the river and village. The home has three comfortable guest rooms—two with jetted tubs—a spacious sitting room, and wireless Internet throughout. A healthy cooked or continental breakfast is included in the rates.

Bragg Creek Shopping Centre holds a wide variety of eateries as well as most services, including a gas station, bakery, grocery store, and post office. Around the corner, at the main intersection, is the **Cinnamon Spoon** (Bragg Creek Trading Post II, 403/949-4110, Mon.–Fri. 6 A.M.–5 P.M., Sat.–Sun. 6 A.M.–5 P.M.), with the best coffee in town, as well as pastries, cakes, smoothies, and sandwiches made to order. At the **Steak Pit** (43 White Ave., 403/949-3633, daily from 11:30 A.M., $24–36), the setting is early Canadian, yet elegant. Eating here isn't cheap but *is* comparable to Calgary restaurants. The menu sets out to prove great steaks don't necessitate fancy trimmings, and does so with the best cuts of Alberta beef and great spuds.

Kananaskis Country

During Alberta's oil-and-gas boom of the 1970s, oil revenues collected by the provincial government were channeled into various projects aimed at improving the lifestyle of Albertans. One lasting legacy of the boom is Kananaskis Country (pronounced Can-AN-a-skiss), a sprawling 4,250-square-kilometer (1,640-square-mile) wilderness area west of Calgary that has been developed with an emphasis on providing recreation opportunities for as many people as possible. Although Kananaskis Country lacks the famous lakes and glaciated peaks of Banff and Jasper National Parks, in many ways it rivals them. Wildlife is abundant, and opportunities for observation of larger mammals are superb.

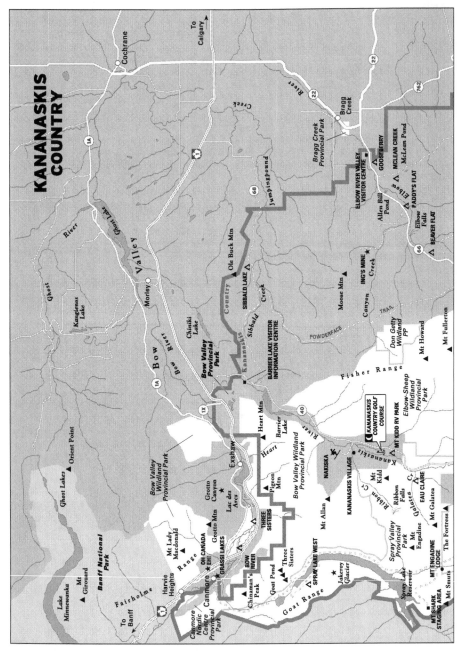

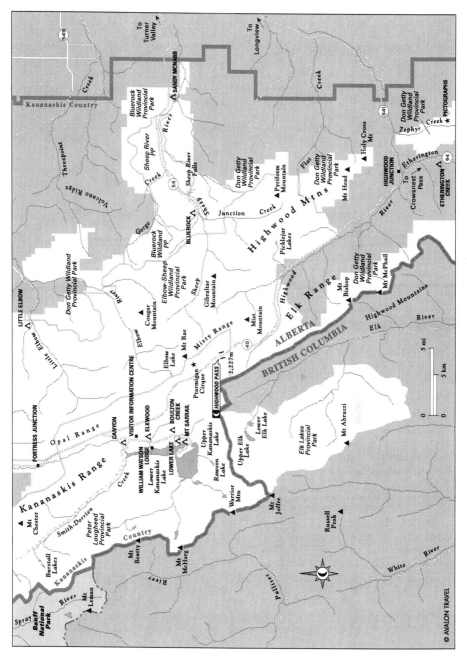

© AVALON TRAVEL

The region has large populations of moose, mule and white-tailed deer, elk, black bears, bighorn sheep, and mountain goats. Wolves, grizzly bears, and cougars are present, too, but are less likely to be seen.

Access and Information

The main access to Kananaskis Country is 80 kilometers (50 miles) west of Calgary off the TransCanada Highway. Other points of access are south from Canmore, at Bragg Creek on the region's east border, or west from Longview in the southeast.

For more information, contact the Tourism, Parks and Recreation office of the provincial government (403/678-5508, www.tpr.alberta.ca/parks). Another good source of information is **Friends of Kananaskis Country** (www.kananaskis.org), a nonprofit organization that advertises educational programs, is involved in a variety of hands-on projects, and promotes Kananaskis Country in partnership with the government.

BOW VALLEY PROVINCIAL PARK

This park, at the north end of Kananaskis Country, sits at the confluence of the Kananaskis and Bow Rivers and extends as far south as Barrier Lake. The entrance to the park is four kilometers (2.5 miles) west of Highway 40 (the main access into Kananaskis Country). To the casual motorist driving along the TransCanada Highway, the park seems fairly small, but more than 300 species of plants have been recorded, and 60 species of birds are known to nest within its boundaries. The abundance of wildflowers, birds, and smaller mammals can be enjoyed along four short interpretive trails. Other popular activities in the park include fishing for a variety of trout and whitefish in the Bow River, bicycling along the paved trail system, and attending interpretive programs presented by park staff.

Practicalities

Facilities at the two park campgrounds, **Willow Rock** and **Bow Valley,** are excellent. They both have showers, flush toilets, and kitchen shelters. Willow Rock also has powered sites and a coin laundry and is open for winter camping. Unserviced sites are $25, powered sites $30. Reservations can be made online for both campgrounds at www.bowvalleycampgrounds.com.

A **visitor information center** (403/673-2163, Mon.–Fri. 8 A.M.–8 P.M. in summer, Mon.–Fri. 8:15 A.M.–4:30 P.M. the rest of the year) is at the park entrance on Highway 1X.

KANANASKIS VALLEY

This is the most developed area of Kananaskis Country, yet summer crowds are minimal compared to Banff.

Sights and Drives

The following sights are along Highway 40 and are detailed from the TransCanada Highway in the north to Peter Lougheed Provincial Park in the south. Your first stop should be **Canoe Meadows,** a large day-use area above the sparkling Kananaskis River. Below the picnic area, white-water enthusiasts use a short stretch of river as a slalom course. Man-made obstacles and gates challenge recreational and racing kayakers, while upstream (around the first bend), the Green Tongue creates a steep wave, allowing kayakers to remain in one spot, spinning and twisting while water rushes past them. South of Canoe Meadows is **Barrier Lake Visitor Information Centre** (403/673-3985, daily 9 A.M.–6 P.M. June–mid-Sept., daily 9 A.M.–4 P.M. the rest of the year). Nestled between Highway 40 and the Kananaskis River, riverside trails lead in both directions, including two kilometers (1.2 miles) downstream to Canoe Meadows. Barrier Lake itself is farther along Highway 40, dominated to the south by the impressive peak of Mount Baldy (2,212 m/7,257 ft). The lake is human-made but still a picture of beauty. From the south end of Barrier Lake, Highway 40 continues south to a spot that will be of particular interest to anglers, **Mount Lorette Ponds,** stocked annually with rainbow trout.

Kananaskis Village lies just off Highway 40

four kilometers (2.5 miles) south of the ponds. The village, the epicenter of action during the 1988 Winter Olympic Games, sits on a high bench below Nakiska—where the downhill events of the games were held—and overlooks a golf course. The village comprises two hotels, restaurants, and other service shops set around a paved courtyard complete with waterfalls and trout-stocked ponds.

From the village, it's 15 kilometers (9.3 miles) farther south to the border of Peter Lougheed Provincial Park. Just beyond the village is **Wedge Pond**. Originally dug as a gravel pit during golf course construction, it is now filled with water and encircled by a one-kilometer (0.6-mile) trail offering fantastic views to towering 2,958-meter (9,700-foot) Mount Kidd.

◖ Kananaskis Country Golf Course

Regularly voted Best Value in North America by *Golf Digest,* this 36-hole layout (403/591-7272 or 877/591-2525, www.kananaskisgolf.com) is bisected by the Kananaskis River and surrounded by magnificent mountain peaks. It comprises two 18-hole courses: **Mount Kidd,** featuring undulating terrain and an island green on the 197-yard fourth hole, and the shorter (which is a relative term—both courses measure over 7,000 yards from the back markers) **Mount Lorette,** where water comes into play on 13 holes. Greens fees are $90 (Albertan residents pay $70) and a cart is an additional $16 per person. Golfers enjoy complimentary valet parking and use of the driving range, as well as a restaurant and bar with awesome mountain views, and a well-stocked golf shop.

Winter Recreation

Nakiska (403/591-7777 or 800/258-7669, www.skinakiska.com) is a state-of-the-art alpine resort built to host the alpine skiing events of the 1988 Winter Olympic Games. Great cruising and fast fall-line skiing on runs cut specially for racing will satisfy the intermediate-to-advanced crowd. The resort has a total of 28 runs and a vertical rise of 735 meters (2,410 feet). Lift tickets are adult $64, senior and youth $54, child $28. Check the website for accommodation packages and transportation schedules from Canmore.

The most accessible of Kananaskis Country's 200 kilometers (124 miles) of cross-country trails are in the Ribbon Creek area. Most heavily used are those radiating from Kananaskis Village and those around the base of Nakiska. Most trails are easy to intermediate, including a five-kilometer (3.1-mile) track up Ribbon Creek. Rentals are available in the Village Trading Post in Kananaskis Village.

Kananaskis Village

Built for the 1988 Winter Olympic Games, Kananaskis Village is home to 412-room **Delta Lodge at Kananaskis** (1 Centennial Road, Kananaskis Village, off of Hwy. 40, 403/591-7711 or 866/432-4322, www.deltahotels.com; from $240 s or d), part of an upscale Canadian hotel chain. It offers three distinct types of rooms in three buildings surrounding a cobbled courtyard. In the main lodge are 251 moderately large Delta rooms, many with mountain views, balconies, and fireplaces. Connected by a covered walkway are 70 Signature Club (a Delta designation) rooms, each boasting elegant Victorian-era charm, a mountain view, a luxurious bathroom complete with bathrobes, oversized beds, and many extras, such as CD players. Guests in this wing also enjoy a private lounge and continental breakfast. Rooms in Mount Kidd Manor combine natural colors with dramatic contemporary styling; some are bedroom lofts with gas fireplaces, kitchenettes, large bathrooms, and sitting rooms. Outdoor seating from various eateries spills into the courtyard and biking and hiking trails radiate out in all directions. All in all, a good place to base yourself for an overnight hotel stay.

The Delta Lodge (403/591-7711) contains three restaurants, a deli, and two bars. For a warm, relaxed atmosphere, head to the **Bighorn Lounge** (daily from 11 A.M.), near the arcade's main entrance. **Obsessions Deli** (daily from 8 A.M.) serves up light snacks, including healthy sandwiches and handmade truffles. Also in the arcade is the **Fireweed Grill** (daily 6 A.M.–10 P.M., $17–31), with a casual Western-style atmosphere, floor-to-ceiling windows, and an adjoining outdoor patio used during summer. **Seasons Steakhouse** (June–Oct. Tues.–Sat. 6–9:30 P.M., $26–39), in the Signature Club wing, is the village's most elegant restaurant.

Other Accommodations and Camping

A magnet for families, the privately owned **[Sundance Lodges** (403/591-7122, www.sundancelodges.com, mid-May–Sept.) is a wonderful option for travelers looking to try camping or who want something a little more adventurous than a regular motel room. Campsites cost $28 per night, with rentals including tents, camp stoves, sleeping bags, and utensil kits available for minimal charge. Next up are the tepees ($57–77), 12 of them, each with colorfully painted canvas walls rising from wooden floors. Inside are mattresses, a heater, and a lantern. Finally, you can stay in one of 18 Trapper Tents ($79 s or d), which are larger but have similar interior fittings and a canvas-covered awning over a picnic table. When you tire of hiking and biking on surrounding trails, return to the lodge for fishing in a man-made pond, horseshoes, badminton, and volleyball. Other amenities include a general store, hot showers, a laundry, and Internet access. Sundance sits beside the Kananaskis River, just off Highway 40, 22 kilometers (13.7 miles) south of the TransCanada Highway.

Mount Kidd RV Park (403/591-7700, www.mountkiddrv.com, unserviced sites $32.50, hookups $41–48, booking fee $8) is a commercial campground along Highway 40 south of Kananaskis Village and the golf course. The campground's showpiece is the Campers Center, containing the main registration area and all the usual bathroom facilities as well as whirlpools, saunas, a wading pool, a game room, a lounge, groceries, a concession area, and a laundry room. Outside are two tennis courts, picnic areas by the river, and many paved biking and hiking trails. Those who can survive without such luxuries should continue 6.5 kilometers (four miles) south to **Eau Claire Campground** (mid-May–early Sept., $20), operated by Kananaskis Camping (403/591-7226, www.kananaskiscamping.com).

PETER LOUGHEED PROVINCIAL PARK

This park is a southern extension of the Kananaskis Valley and protects the upper watershed of the Kananaskis River. It is contained within a high mountain valley and dominated by two magnificent bodies of water—**Upper** and **Lower Kananaskis Lakes.** The 500-square-kilometer (193-square-mile) wilderness is the second-largest provincial park in Alberta.

Highway 40 is the main route through the park. The most important intersection to make note of is five kilometers (3.1 miles) along Highway 40 from the park's north boundary. At this point, Kananaskis Lakes Road branches off to the west, accessing Upper and Lower Kananaskis Lakes. These two lakes are the center of boating and fishing in the park, and opportunities abound for hiking and camping nearby.

[Highwood Pass

In the southeastern corner of the park, Highway 40 climbs to Highwood Pass (2,227 m/7,310 ft), the highest road pass in Canada. On the way up to the pass, a pleasant detour is Valley View Trail, a five-kilometer (3.1-mile) paved wooden route higher up the slopes of the Opal Range allows views across the entire park to the Continental Divide. The pass itself is right at the tree line, one of the most accessible alpine areas in all the Canadian Rockies. Simply step out of your vehicle and follow the interpretive trails through the **Highwood Meadows.** In the vicinity, the **Rock Glacier Trail,** two kilometers (1.2 miles) north of Highwood Pass, leads 150 meters (0.1 miles) to a unique formation of moraine rock.

From the pass, Highway 40 descends into the Highwood/Cataract Creek areas of

Kananaskis Country (Highwood Junction is 35 km/22 mi from the pass). **Note:** The road over the Highwood Pass is in a critical wildlife habitat and is closed December 1–June 15.

Hiking

The park offers a number of interesting interpretive trails and more strenuous hikes. Most trailheads are along Kananaskis Lakes Road, a paved road that leads off Highway 40 to Upper and Lower Kananaskis Lakes. **Rockwall Trail,** from the Visitor Information Centre, and **Marl Lake Trail,** from Elkwood Campground, are wheelchair accessible and barrier-free, respectively. The **Boulton Creek Trail** (4.9 km/three mi, 90 minutes round-trip) is an easy loop that begins from Boulton Bridge, 10 kilometers (6.2 miles) from Highway 40. A booklet, available at the trailhead, corresponds with numbered posts along this interpretive trail.

From the Upper Lake day-use area, at the very end of Kananaskis Lakes Road, the trail to **Rawson Lake** (3.5 km/2.2 mi, 1.5 hours one-way) begins by following the lakeshore for just over one kilometer (0.6-mile). Just beyond the small waterfall it begins an uphill climb (305 m/1,000 ft), ending at a picturesque subalpine lake surrounded by a towering, yet magnificently symmetrical, headwall. The setting of **Elbow Lake** (1.3 km/0.8 mi, 30 minutes one-way) is almost as spectacular as Rawson, but the trail is shorter (and therefore busier). The trailhead is the Elbow Pass day-use area, beside Highway 40, 13 kilometers (eight miles) south of Kananaskis Lakes Road. Continue south along Highway 40 to Highwood Pass (four km/2.5 mi) to the **Ptarmigan Cirque Trail** (5.6 km/3.5 mi, 2 hours round-trip), a steep (elevation gain is 230 m/750 ft) interpretive walk that climbs high into the treeless alpine zone. Along the way you're likely to see numerous small mammals—Columbian ground squirrels, pikas, least chipmunks, and hoary marmots are all common.

Other Recreation

The **Bike Trail** is a 20-kilometer (12.5-mile) paved trail designed especially for bicycles that begins behind the Visitor Information Centre and follows Lower Kananaskis Lake to Mount Sarrail Campground. Many other trails are designated for mountain-biking use; inquire at the Visitor Information Centre (403/591-6344). **Boulton Creek Trading Post** (403/591-7058) rents mountain bikes during summer. Upper and Lower Kananaskis Lakes have fair fishing for a variety of trout and whitefish. A nightly interpretive program takes place in campground amphitheaters throughout the park. Look for schedules posted on bulletin boards, or check with the Visitor Information Centre.

Camping

Within the park are six auto-accessible campgrounds that hold a total of 507 sites. All are on Kananaskis Lakes Road and are linked by bicycle and hiking trails. **Boulton Creek Campground** ($22–34) has coin-operated showers just beyond the registration gate (complete with rack for those who have a bike), flush toilets, a few of the 118 sites with power, and an interpretive amphitheater, and is within walking distance of a restaurant and grocery store. **Elkwood Campground** ($20) is the largest of the park's campgrounds, with 130 sites. It offers showers ($1 for five minutes) along each of four loops, flush toilets, a playground, and an interpretive amphitheater. **Canyon, Lower Lakes,** and **ⓒ Interlakes Campgrounds** ($20) are more rustic, with only pit toilets, pump water, and picnic tables (Interlakes has some great water-view sites). **Mt. Sarrail Campground** ($20) is described as a "walk-in" campground for tenters, but some sites are right by the main parking lot. All campgrounds in Peter Lougheed Provincial Park are operated by Kananaskis Camping Inc. (403/591-7226, www.kananaskiscamping.com).

Information and Services

At the excellent Visitor Information Centre (four km/2.5 mi along Kananaskis Lakes Rd. from Hwy. 40, 403/591-6322, summer daily 9 A.M.–7 P.M., the rest of the year Mon.–Fri. 9 A.M.–5 P.M. and weekends 9 A.M.–5 P.M.), exhibits catalog the natural and cultural history of the park through photographs, videos, and hands-on displays. The knowledgeable staff hides hordes of literature under the desk—you have to ask for it. A large lounge area that overlooks the valley to the Opal Range is used mainly in winter by cross-country skiers but is always open for trip planning or relaxing.

Located along Kananaskis Lakes Road, 10 kilometers (6.2 mi) south of Highway 40, **Boulton Creek Trading Post** is the park's only commercial center. It sells groceries, basic camping supplies, fishing tackle and licenses, propane, and firewood. Adjacent is an unremarkable family-style restaurant serving up pasta, burgers, and the like. A cooked breakfast is $10 (although it's not open until 9 A.M.). It also has an ice-cream window and serves coffee.

SPRAY VALLEY PROVINCIAL PARK

The creation of 35,800-hectare (88,460-acre) Spray Valley Provincial Park in 2001 provided the final link in continuous protection between bordering Peter Lougheed Provincial Park in the south and Willmore Wilderness Park beyond the northern reaches of Jasper National Park in the north. The park's dominant feature is **Spray Lake Reservoir,** a 16-kilometer-long (10-mile-long) body of water that provides a variety of recreational opportunities.

The **Smith-Dorrien/Spray Trail** is the only road through the park. This 60-kilometer (37-mile) unpaved (and often dusty) road links Peter Lougheed Provincial Park in the south to Canmore in the north. From the south, the road climbs up the Smith-Dorrien Creek watershed, passing Mud Lake and entering the Spray Valley Provincial Park just south of Mt. Engadine Lodge. Around three kilometers (1.9 miles) farther north is **Buller Pond** (on the west side of the road), from where the distinctive "Matterhorn" peak of Mount Assiniboine can be seen on a clear day. The road then parallels the eastern shoreline of Spray Lake for over 20 kilometers (12.5 miles), passing three lakefront picnic areas. Beyond the north end of Spray Lake, the road passes **Goat Pond** and the Goat Creek trailhead, then descends steeply into the Bow Valley and Canmore.

Accommodations and Camping

◖ **Mount Engadine Lodge** (403/678-4080, www.mountengadine.com, mid-June–mid-Oct. Jan. weekends, Feb.–March; from $190 s, $390–440 d including meals) is set on a ridge overlooking an open meadow and small creek at the turnoff to the Mount Shark staging area. It comprises luxurious rooms in the main lodge and two cabins set on a ridge overlooking an open meadow and small creek. The main lodge has a dining room, a comfortable lounge area with two stone fireplaces, and a beautiful sundeck holding a hot tub. Breakfast is served buffet-style, lunch can be taken at the lodge or packed for a picnic, and dinner is served in multiple courses of hearty European specialties. Mount Engadine Lodge is 40 kilometers (25 miles) southwest of Canmore, at the turnoff to the Mount Shark staging area.

The park's only campground is **Spray Lake West** (June–Sept., $20), a rustic facility spread out along the western shoreline of Spray Lake. Many of the 50-odd sites are very private, but facilities are limited to picnic tables, fire pits, and pit toilets.

SIBBALD

The Sibbald Creek Trail (Hwy. 68) traverses the rolling foothills of the Sibbald and Jumpingpound Valleys and is accessible from the TransCanada Highway, intersecting Highway 40 south of the Barrier Lake Visitor Information Centre. Fishing is popular in **Sibbald Lake** and **Sibbald Meadows Pond.** A couple of short trails begin at the picnic area at Sibbald Lake, including the 4.4-kilometer (2.7-mile) **Ole Buck Loop,** which climbs a low ridge.

Sibbald Lake Campground offers 134 sites spread around five loops (Loop D comes closest to the lake). Amenities include pit toilets, drinking water, and a nightly interpretive program; $24 per site. For camping information contact Elbow Valley Campgrounds (403/949-3132, www.evcamp.com).

BIGHORN SHEEP

Bighorn sheep are the most distinctive of the hoofed mammals in western Canada. Easily recognized by their impressive horns, they're often seen grazing on grassy mountain slopes or at salt licks beside the road. The color of their coat varies with the season; in summer it's a brownish gray with a cream-colored belly and rump, turning lighter in winter. Males can weigh up to 120 kilograms (265 pounds). Females generally weigh around 80 kilograms (180 pounds). Both sexes possess horns, rather than antlers like moose, elk, and deer. Unlike antlers, horns are not shed each year and can grow to astounding sizes. The horns of rams are larger than those of ewes and curve up to 360 degrees. The spiraled horns of an older ram can measure over one meter (three feet) and weigh as much as 15 kilograms (33 pounds). In fall, during the mating season, a hierarchy is established among these animals for the right to breed ewes. As the males face off against each other to establish dominance, their horns act as both a weapon and a buffer against the head-butting of other rams. The skull structure of the bighorn, rams in particular, has become adapted to these clashes, preventing heavy concussion.

These animals are particularly tolerant of humans and often approach parked vehicles; although they are not dangerous, as with all mammals in the park, you should not approach or feed them.

ELBOW RIVER VALLEY

The main access road into the Elbow River Valley is Highway 66 west from Bragg Creek. It climbs steadily along the Elbow River, passing **McLean Pond** and **Allen Bill Pond** (both are stocked with rainbow trout) and six-meter-high (20-foot-high) **Elbow Falls**, before climbing through an area devastated by wildfire in 1981, then descending to a campground 42 kilometers (26 miles) from Bragg Creek.

Five campgrounds with a combined total of 551 sites lie along the Elbow River Valley. The most developed of the five is **McLean Creek Campground,** 12 kilometers (7.5 miles) west of Bragg Creek. At the campground entrance is the Camper Centre with groceries, coin showers, and firewood ($6 per bundle). Unpowered sites are $25 per night, powered sites $32. For reservations contact Elbow Valley Campgrounds (403/949-3132, www.evcamp. com). The other campgrounds and their distances from Bragg Creek are **Gooseberry** (10 km/6.2 mi), **Paddy's Flat** (20 km/12.4 mi), **Beaver Flat** (30 km/18.6 mi), and, at the very end of the road, **Little Elbow** (50 km/31 mi). Each of these campgrounds has only basic facilities—pit toilets and hand-pumped drinking water—but, still, sites are $24 per night.

SHEEP RIVER VALLEY

The Sheep River Valley lies immediately south of the Elbow River Valley, in an area of rolling foothills between open ranchlands to the east and the high peaks bordering **Elbow-Sheep Wildland Provincial Park** to the west. Access is from the town of Turner Valley (take Sunset Blvd. west from downtown), along Highway 546. The highway passes through **Sheep River Provincial Park** (which protects the wintering ground of bighorn sheep) and **Sheep River Falls,** and ends at a campground 46 kilometers (29 miles) west of Turner Valley.

Along Highway 546, west from Turner Valley, are two campgrounds. **Sandy McNabb Campround** (403/558-2373 or 866/366-2267, www.campingalberta.com, $20), the larger of the two, is a pleasant walk from the river right by the entrance to Kananaskis Country. All sites are filled on a first-come, first-served basis.

HIGHWOOD AND CATARACT CREEK

The Highwood/Cataract Creek areas stretch from Peter Lougheed Provincial Park to the southern border of Kananaskis Country. This is the least developed area in Kananaskis Country. The jagged peaks of the Highwood

Mountains, mostly protected by remote **Don Getty Wildland Provincial Park** are the dominant feature; high alpine meadows among the peaks are home to bighorn sheep, elk, and grizzlies. Lower down, spruce and lodgepole pine forests spread over most of the valley, giving way to grazing lands along the eastern flanks. The main access from the north is along Highway 40, which drops 600 vertical meters (1,970 feet) in the 35 kilometers (22 miles) between **Highwood Pass** and **Highwood Junction.** From the east, Highway 541 west from Longview joins Highway 40 at Highwood Junction.

All three campgrounds in the Highwood/Cataract Creek areas are south of Highwood Junction and are operated by High Country Camping (403/558-2373 or 866/366-2267, www.campingalberta.com).

Canmore

The town of Canmore (12,500) lies in the Bow Valley, 103 kilometers (64 miles) west of Calgary, 28 kilometers (17 miles) southeast of Banff, and on the northern edge of Kananaskis Country. Long perceived as a gateway to the mountain national parks, the town is very much a destination in itself these days. Its ideal mountain location and the freedom it enjoys from the strict development restrictions that apply in the nearby parks have made Canmore the fastest-growing town in Canada, with the population having tripled in the last 20 years. The surrounding mountains provide Canmore's best recreation opportunities. Hiking is excellent on trails that lace the valley and mountainside slopes, with many high viewpoints easily reached. Flowing though town, the Bow River offers great fishing, kayaking, and rafting; golfers flock to three scenic courses; and nearby Mount Yamnuska has become the most developed rock-climbing site in the Canadian Rockies. Canmore also hosted the Nordic events of the 1988 Winter Olympic Games and is the home of the Alpine Club of Canada.

SIGHTS AND RECREATION

Canmore is spread across both sides of the TransCanada Highway, with downtown Canmore occupying an island in the middle of the Bow River. Although development sprawls in all directions, large tracts of forest remain intact, including along the river, where you'll find paths leading beyond built-up areas and into natural areas. The most expansive of these is 32,600-hectare (80,550-acre) **Bow Valley Wildland Provincial Park,** which has been designated in pockets along the valley floor as well as most of the surrounding mountain slopes along both sides of the valley.

Downtown

The downtown core of Canmore, on the southwestern side of the TransCanada Highway, has managed to retain much of its original charm. Many historical buildings line the downtown streets, while other buildings from the coal-mining days are being preserved at their original locations around town. The first building of interest at the east end of the main street is Canmore's original **NWMP post** (609 8th St., 403/678-1955, summer daily 9 A.M.–6 P.M., the rest of the year Mon.–Fri. noon–4 P.M., free), built in 1892. It is one of the few such posts still in its original position, even though at the time of its construction the building was designed as a temporary structure to serve the newly born coal-mining town. The interior is decorated with period furnishings, while out back is a thriving garden filled with the same food crops planted by the post's original inhabitants.

Just off the main street, inside the impressive Civic Centre complex, is **Canmore Museum and Geoscience Centre** (902 7th Ave., 403/678-2462, Mon.–Tues. noon–5 P.M., Wed.–Sun. 10 A.M.–6 P.M., adult $3, senior and child $2). This facility highlights the

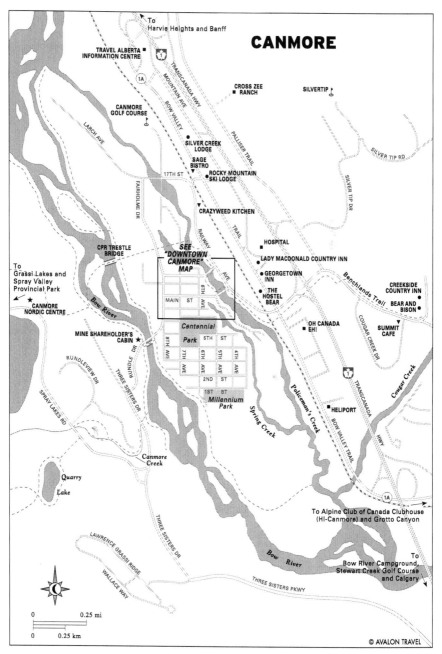

CANMORE

To Harvie Heights and Banff

TRAVEL ALBERTA INFORMATION CENTRE

CROSS ZEE RANCH

SILVERTIP

CANMORE GOLF COURSE

SILVER TIP RD

SILVER CREEK LODGE

SAGE BISTRO

ROCKY MOUNTAIN SKI LODGE

17TH ST

SILVER TIP DR

CRAZYWEED KITCHEN

HOSPITAL

SEE "DOWNTOWN CANMORE" MAP

CPR TRESTLE BRIDGE

LADY MACDONALD COUNTRY INN

GEORGETOWN INN

CREEKSIDE COUNTRY INN

To Grassi Lakes and Spray Valley Provincial Park

THE HOSTEL BEAR

BEAR AND BISON

CANMORE NORDIC CENTRE

MAIN ST

6TH AVE

SUMMIT CAFE

OH CANADA EH!

MINE SHAREHOLDER'S CABIN

Centennial Park

8TH AVE

5TH ST

7TH AVE

6TH AVE

5TH AVE

4TH AVE

2ND ST

1ST ST

Millennium Park

HELIPORT

Bow River

RUNDLEVIEW DR

RUNDLE DR

THREE SISTERS DR

SPRAY LAKES RD

Canmore Creek

Spring Creek

Policeman's Creek

BOW VALLEY TRAIL

TRANSCANADA HWY

COUGAR CREEK DR

BENCHLANDS TRAIL

Cougar Creek

Quarry Lake

LAWRENCE GRASSI RIDGE

THREE SISTERS DR

WALLACE WAY

Bow River

THREE SISTERS PKWY

To Alpine Club of Canada Clubhouse (HI-Canmore) and Grotto Canyon

To Bow River Campground, Stewart Creek Golf Course and Calgary

LARCH AVE

FAIRHOLME DR

MOUNTAIN AVE

BOW VALLEY TRAIL

TRANSCANADA HWY

RAILWAY AVE

PALLISER TRAIL

0   0.25 mi

0   0.25 km

© AVALON TRAVEL

region's rich geological history and its importance to the growth of the town and related industries.

Canmore Nordic Centre

This sprawling complex on the outskirts of Canmore was built for the 1988 Winter Olympic Games. The cross-country skiing and biathlon (combined cross-country skiing and rifle shooting) events were held here, and today the center remains a world-class training ground for Canadian athletes in a variety of disciplines. Even in summer, long after the snow has melted, the place is worth a visit. An interpretive trail leads down to and along the west bank of the Bow River to the barely visible remains of Georgetown, a once-bustling coal-mining town. Many other trails lead around the grounds, and it's possible to hike or bike along the Bow River all the way to Banff. **Mountain biking** is extremely popular on 70 kilometers

(43.5 miles) of trails. Bike rentals are available at **Trail Sports** (below the day lodge, 403/678-6764, daily 9 A.M.–6 P.M.), where rates are $15 per hour and $45 per day for a front-suspension bike, $20 and $60, respectively, for a full-suspension bike. Snowmaking guarantees a ski season running December–late March, with rentals and instruction available through Trail Sports.

Hiking

Paved paths around town are suitable for walking and biking. They link Policeman's Creek with the golf course, Nordic center, and Riverview Park on the Bow River. To explore the surrounding wilderness, consider one of the following longer walks.

The historic **Grassi Lakes Trail** (two km/1.2 mi, 40 minutes one-way) begins from just off Spray Lakes Road, one kilometer (0.6 miles) beyond the Nordic center. Around 150 meters

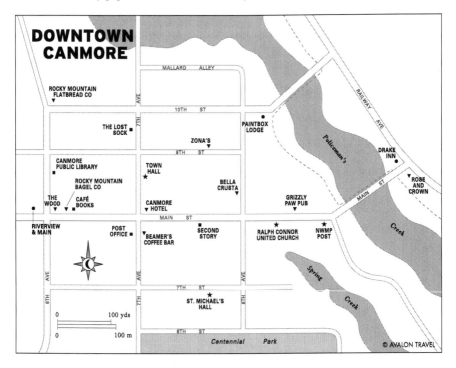

Canmore Nordic Centre

(0.1 miles) from the parking lot, take the left fork. From this point, the trail climbs steadily to stairs cut into a cliff face before leading up to a bridge over Canmore Creek and to the two small lakes. With Chinaman's Peak as a backdrop, these gin-clear, spring-fed lakes are a particularly rewarding destination. Behind the upper lake, an easy scramble up a scree slope leads to four pictographs (native rock paintings) of human figures. They're on the first large boulder in the gorge.

Across the valley, the parking lot at Benchlands Trail and Elk Run Boulevard is the beginning of two trails. One follows **Cougar Creek** into a narrow valley. The first section of trail runs alongside a man-made channel that acts as a conduit for run-off in years of high snowfall (the "creek" is dry all summer). The rough trail then enters a canyon and crosses the creekbed 10 times in the first three kilometers (1.9 miles) to a major fork (allow one hour), which is a fine turnaround point. Where Cougar Creek exits the canyon, look for a faint trail winding up a grassy bank to the left. It leads up **Mount Lady Macdonald** (3.5 km/2.1

mi, 90 minutes one-way), gaining a strenuous 850 meters (2,790 feet) of elevation along the way. The distance given is to a disused helipad below the main summit. It's a steep, unrelenting slog, but views across the Bow Valley are stunning. From this point, the true summit is another 275 vertical meters (900 feet) away, along an extremely narrow ridge that drops away precipitously to the east.

Golf

As with golfing elsewhere in the Canadian Rockies, book all tee times well in advance, but also try to be flexible, because two of Canmore's three courses offer weekday and twilight discounts. **Silvertip** (2000 Silvertip Trail, 403/678-1600 or 877/877-5444, greens fee $175) spreads across a series of wide benches between the valley floor and the lower slopes of Mount Lady Macdonald. The layout is challenging, with the most distinct feature being an elevation change of 200 meters (660 feet) between the lowest and highest points on the course. **Stewart Creek Golf Club** (4100 Stewart Creek Dr., 403/609-6099 or 877/993-

4653, www.stewartcreekgolf.com, $175–195), another newer layout, is made more interesting by hanging greens, greenside exposed rock, and historic mine shafts. **Canmore Golf & Curling Club** (2000 8th Ave., 403/678-4785, $114) is an 18-hole course is an interesting layout, with scenic panoramas and water on some holes.

Horseback Riding
Nestled on a wide bench on the northeastern side of town, **Cross Zee Ranch** (403/678-4171) has been guiding visitors through the valley since the 1950s. From expansive stables, rides pass through thickly wooded areas, along colorful meadows, and to high lookouts. Options include Ranger Ridge and Bone Gully (one hour, $38 per person), Sunny Bench (90 minutes, $52), and the Great Aspens ride (two hours, $68).

ENTERTAINMENT AND EVENTS
Nightlife
Oh Canada Eh! (125 Kananaskis Way, off Bow Valley Trail, 403/609-0004 or 800/773-0004) is a musical dinner show that provides a rip-roaring evening of fun and food in a modern building decorated as a cavernous log cabin. It's unashamedly cheesy, but the parade of costumed Canadian characters—such as lumberjacks, natives, Mounties, and even Anne of Green Gables—will keep you laughing as they sing and dance across the floor. The food is surprisingly good, with Canadian favorites such as Alberta beef, salmon, and maple chocolate cake served buffet-style. Performances are nightly at 6:30 P.M. through summer, and the all-inclusive cost is adult $64, child 6–16 $31.

The Wood (838 8th St., 403/678-3404) has a beer garden that catches the afternoon sun and is especially busy on weekends. At the other end of the main street is the **Drake Inn** (909 Railway Ave., 403/678-5131), with a small outdoor patio and a nonsmoking section with comfortable lounges. Across the road, at the **Rose and Crown** (749 Railway Ave., 403/678-5168), you'll find a beer garden. All these bars have midweek drink specials, and the latter two have a couple of pool tables.

Festivals and Events
Canmore's small-town pride lives on through a busy schedule of festivals and events, which are nearly always accompanied by parades of flag-waving kids, free downtown pancake breakfasts, and an evening shindig somewhere in town.

On the middle weekend of May, it's all about the kids at the **Canmore Children's Festival** (www.canmorechildrensfestival.com), where the fun and frivolity centers on the local high school grounds off 17th Street. Expect lots of music, live theater, story-telling, and educational presentations. **ArtsPeak Arts Festival** (403/678-6436, www.artspeakcanmore.com) is a mid-June celebration hosted at venues throughout town. As the name suggests expect lots of art-oriented festivities, including workshops, displays, and walking tours.

Canada Day is celebrated with a pancake breakfast, parade, various activities in Centennial Park, and 10:30 P.M. fireworks. On the first weekend of August, Canmore hosts a **Folk Music Festival** (www.canmore-folkfestival.com), which starts on Saturday and runs through Monday evening. Canmore Nordic Centre hosts a variety of mountain-biking events each summer, highlighted by a late August stop on the **24 Hours of Adrenalin** tour (www.24hoursofadrenalin.com) in which 1,500 racers complete as many laps as they can in a 24-hour period.

The first Sunday of September is the **Canmore Highland Games** (www.canmore-highlandgames.ca), a day of dancing, eating, and caber tossing, culminating in a spectacular and noisy parade of pipe bands throughout the grounds of Centennial Park. The grand finale is the *ceilidh,* a traditional Scottish celebration involving loud beer-drinking, foot-stomping music, which takes place under a massive tent set up in the park for the occasion. Fall's other major gathering is for the **Festival of the Eagles** (www.eaglewatch.ca), on the middle weekend of October and coinciding with the southbound migration of golden eagles.

ACCOMMODATIONS AND CAMPING

Canmore's population boom has been mirrored by the construction of new hotels and motels. Most of the newer lodgings are on Bow Valley Trail (Hwy. 1A). As with all resort towns in the Canadian Rockies, reservations should be made as far in advance as possible in summer.

Under $50

HI-Canmore (403/678-3200, www.hihostels. ca, dorms $30–36, private rooms $60–81) is an excellent hostel-style accommodation at the base of Grotto Mountain. Affiliated with Hostelling International, the lodge is part of headquarters for the Alpine Club of Canada, the country's national mountaineering organization. In addition to sleeping up to 46 people in seven rooms, it has a kitchen, an excellent library, a laundry room, a bar, a sauna, and a lounge area with a fireplace. To get there from downtown, follow Bow Valley Trail southeast; it's signposted to the left, 500 meters (0.3 mile) after passing under the TransCanada Highway.

Built as a motel, **The Hostel Bear** (1002 Bow Valley Trail, 403/678-1000 or 888/678-1008, www.thehostelbear.com; dorms $32, from $84 s or d) is now a beautiful facility for budget travelers. It features eye-catching timber and river-stone styling outside and an impressive lobby. Amenities include a living area with an LCD TV and fireplace, a large modern kitchen, a laundry, wireless Internet, and comfortable beds for 170 guests, with configurations ranging from 10-bed dorms to private en suite rooms.

$100-150

With around $100 budgeted for a room, it's hard to pass up **Riverview and Main,** centrally located half a block beyond the end of the downtown core (918 8th St., 403/678-9777, www.riverviewandmain.com, $115 s, $135 d). The rooms are decently sized and brightly decorated, and each has access to a deck. The guest lounge centers on a river-stone, wood-burning fireplace. Rates include a selection of hot and cold breakfast items.

Not only can you rent one- and two-bedroom units with full kitchens at **Rocky Mountain Ski Lodge** (1711 Bow Valley Trail, 403/678-5445 or 800/665-6111, www.rockymtnskilodge.com, from $129 s or d), there's plenty of outdoor space for kids to run around, including a small playground. Also on the property is a barbecue and picnic area, a laundry, and wireless Internet. The self-contained suites, some with loft bedrooms, cost from $169.

At the edge of Canmore's downtown core is the **Drake Inn** (909 Railway Ave., 403/678-5131 or 800/461-8730, www.drakeinn.com, from $129 s, $139 d). It offers bright and cheerfully decorated motel rooms. Well worth an extra $10 are Creekside Rooms, featuring private balconies overlooking Policeman's Creek. The adjoining bar opens daily at 7 A.M. for the best-value breakfast in town.

$150-200

Silver Creek Lodge (1818 Mountain Ave., 403/678-4242 or 877/598-4242, www.silvercreekcanmore.ca, $159–289 s or d) provides hotel and suite accommodations within a much larger condominium development. Aside from modern kitchen-equipped rooms, many with mountain views, highlights include the highly recommended Wild Orchid Asian Bistro, spa services, outdoor hot tubs, and underground parking.

Lady Macdonald Country Inn (1201 Bow Valley Trail, 403/678-3665 or 800/567-3919, www.ladymacdonald.com, $160–250 s or d) exudes a welcoming atmosphere and personalized service not experienced in the larger properties. Its 12 rooms are all individually furnished, with the smallest, the Palliser Room, featuring elegant surroundings and a magnificent wrought-iron bed. Rates include a hearty hot breakfast in a country-style breakfast room.

Creekside Country Inn (709 Benchlands Trail, 403/609-5522 or 866/609-5522, www. creeksidecountryinn.com, $159–239 s or d) is a modern mountain-style lodge featuring lots of exposed timber. The 12 rooms are elegant in their simplicity; eight have lofts. Facilities include a lounge with roaring log fire, a small exercise room, a whirlpool, and a steam room. Rates include a gourmet continental breakfast that will set you up for the day.

Named for one of the valley's original coal-mining communities, the **◖ Georgetown Inn** (1101 Bow Valley Trail, 403/678-3439 or 866/695-5955, www.georgetowninn.ca; $169-230 s or d) is set up as a country inn of times gone by, complete with a pub-style dining room open daily for breakfast, lunch, and dinner. Each of the 20 guest rooms has its own individual charm, with a modern twist on decor that features lots of English antiques. The best value are Victoria Rooms, each with a separate sitting area and electric fireplace ($159).

Over $200

◖ Bear and Bison (705 Benchlands Trail, 403/678-2058, www.bearandbisoninn.com, $279-329 s or d) is an elegant lodging with nine guest rooms in three different themes. Each room has a king-size four-poster bed, a jetted tub, a fireplace, and a private balcony or patio. Guests enjoy an inviting library and a private garden complete with an oversized hot tub. Rates include baked goods on arrival, pre-dinner drinks, and a breakfast you will remember for a long time.

Paintbox Lodge (629 10th St., 403/609-0482 or 888/678-6100, www.paintboxlodge. com, $209-289 s or d) has the same upscale charm as the Bear and Bison but enjoys a more central location, just one block from the main street. The lobby itself—exposed hand-hewn timbers, slate tiles, and unique pieces of mountain-themed art—is an eye-catching gem. The upscale mountain decor continues through the eight large guest rooms, each lavishly decorated with muted natural colors and a tasteful selection of heritage artifacts.

Camping

East of Canmore are three government campgrounds operated by **Bow Valley Campgrounds** (403/673-2163, www.bowvalleycampgrounds.com). Each has pit toilets, kitchen shelters, and firewood for sale at $8 per bundle. None have hookups. **Bow River Campground** (open late Apr.–early Sept.) is three kilometers (1.9 miles) east of Canmore at the Three Sisters Parkway overpass; **Three Sisters Campground** (mid-Apr.–Oct.) is accessed from Deadman's Flats, a further four kilometers (2.5 miles) east, but it has a pleasant treed setting; **Lac des Arcs Campground** (late Apr.–mid-Sept.) slopes down to the edge of a large lake of the same name seven kilometers (4.3 miles) farther toward Calgary. Sites are $20-22 and reservations are taken from April 1.

FOOD

The restaurant scene has come a long way in Canmore in the last decade. While you can still get inexpensive bar meals at local pubs, other choices run the gamut, from the lively atmosphere of dining in the front yard of a converted residence to Spanish tapas.

Cafés

The **Rocky Mountain Bagel Company** (830 8th St., 403/678-9978, daily 6:30 A.M.–10 P.M.) is a popular early-morning gathering spot. With a central location, it's always busy but manages to maintain an inviting atmosphere. It's the perfect place to start the day with a good strong coffee and fruit-filled muffin. Down one block, **Beamer's Coffee Bar** (737 7th Ave., 403/609-0111, daily 6:30 A.M.–10 P.M.) is a smaller space with equally good coffee.

Away from downtown, near where Cougar Creek enters Canmore from the Fairholme Range, is the **Summit Café** (1001 Cougar Creek Dr., 403/609-2120, daily 6:30 A.M.–6 P.M.; kitchen closes at 4 P.M.). It features a health-conscious menu including lots of salads, but many people come just to soak up the sun on the outside deck or relax with the daily paper and a cup of coffee.

Pizza

Bella Crusta (702 6th Ave., 403/609-3366, Mon.–Sat. 10 A.M.–6 P.M.) is the purveyor of excellent pizza. Heated slices to go are $6, or pay $14-16 for a family-sized version and heat it yourself on a barbecue as the friendly staff recommends.

Off the top end of Main Street, **Rocky Mountain Flatbread Co.** (838 10th St., 403/609-5508; daily 11:30 A.M.–9:30 P.M., $10–16) is a lovely space of natural tones dominated by a clay wood-fired oven in one corner. The oven is also the main attraction when it comes to the food—gourmet flatbread-style pizzas in the $14–20 range. My advice: Start with a bowl of made-from-scratch chicken noodle soup ($6.50), then move on to the chicken, apple, and cheery tomato pizza (the $16.50 size is enough for two people).

Contemporary Canadian

Canmore has seen many top-notch restaurants open in the last few years, but one of the originals, **Zona's** (710 9th St., 403/609-2000, daily 11 A.M.–2 A.M. but for dinner only outside summer, $13–19), remains popular. The food is great, and so is the restaurant itself—earthy tones, hardwood floors, rustic furniture, bamboo blinds, and kiln-fired clay crockery create an inviting ambience unequaled in Canmore.

The menu takes its roots from around the world, with an emphasis on healthy eating and freshly prepared Canadian produce. Choose from dishes such as lamb shepherd's pie or vegetarian korma. A large deck provides much-needed extra seating in summer.

Crazyweed Kitchen (1600 Railway Ave., 403/609-2530, daily 11:30 A.M.–3 P.M. and from 5 P.M., $18–38) dishes up creative culinary fare that gets rave reviews from even cultured Calgarians. From the busy, open kitchen, all manner of creative dishes are on offer—beef short ribs in curry, steamed Alaskan cod, and gourmet pizzas. Healthy portions are served at tables inside or out. Also notable is the extensive wine list, with glasses from $8 and bottles from $38.

Asian

Wild Orchid Bistro (Silver Creek Lodge, 1818 Mountain Ave., 403/679-2029, daily except Tues. for dinner, call for lunch hours, $15–28) is my favorite Japanese restaurant in the Canadian Rockies. It features all the usual choices, all expertly crafted in the open

© ANDREW HEMPSTEAD

Crazyweed Kitchen is one of Canmore's premier restaurants.

kitchen, as well as many with a Western twist. Perfect presentation, mountain views, and a large deck add to the appeal.

INFORMATION AND SERVICES

The best source of pre-trip information (apart from this book, of course) is **Tourism Canmore** (403/678-1295 or 866/226-6673, www.tourismcanmore.com). A **Travel Alberta Information Centre** (403/678-5277, May–Sept. 8 A.M.–8 P.M., Oct. 9 A.M.–6 P.M.) is just off the TransCanada Highway on the west side of town.

The **Rocky Mountain Outlook** and **Canmore Leader** are both filled with local issues and entertainment listings; both are available free on stands throughout the valley. **Canmore Public Library** (950 8th Ave., 403/678-2468, Mon.–Thurs. 11 A.M.–8 P.M., Fri.–Sun. 11 A.M.–5 P.M.) has free Internet access. At the top end of the main street, **Café Books** (826 Main St., 403/678-0908, Mon.–Sat. 10 A.M.–6 P.M., Sun. 10:30 A.M.–5:30 P.M., later hours in summer) stocks an excellent selection of Canadiana. With a huge collection of used books, **Second Story** (713 8th St., 403/609-2368) hasn't been on the second floor since the weight of the books forced a move downstairs to the basement of the same address.

The post office is on 7th Avenue, beside Rusticana Grocery. **The Lost Sock** laundry (in the small mall on 7th Ave. at 10th St.) is open 24 hours daily and has Internet access. **Canmore Hospital** (403/678-5536) is along Bow Valley Trail. For the **RCMP,** call 403/678-5516.

Central Alberta

The boundaries of this region are defined by Calgary in the south, Edmonton to the north, the Canadian Rockies in the west, and the Saskatchewan border in the east. Although it is a large swathe of the province, in this section I make it manageable for visitors by recommending a variety of routes between Alberta's two largest cities.

CALGARY TO ROCKY MOUNTAIN HOUSE

Highway 22 follows the eastern flanks of the foothills from Cochrane, northwest of Calgary, through a string of small communities to Rocky Mountain House.

Sundre

This town of 2,500, on the banks of the Red Deer River, is the quintessential Albertan town. Surrounded by rolling foothills that are historically tied to the ranching industry, oil and gas now keep the local economy alive. In town, Sundre's **Pioneer Village Museum** (130 Centre St., 403/638-3233, May–Oct. Mon. and Wed.–Sat. 10 A.M.–5 P.M., Sun. 1–5 P.M., Nov.–Apr. Wed.–Sat. 10 A.M.–5 P.M., Sun. 1–4 P.M., adult $10, senior and child $8) displays a large collection of artifacts from early pioneer days, including farm machinery, a blacksmith shop, and an old schoolhouse.

The most appealing of Sundre's four motels is the **Chinook Country Inn** (120 2nd St. SW, 403/638-3300, www.chinookcountryinn. ca, $75 s or d), where the rates include a light breakfast. The town-operated **Greenwood Campground** (403/638-2130, mid-May–late Sept., unserviced sites $20, hookups $25–30), on the west bank of the Red Deer River within walking distance of downtown, has clean facilities that include showers and a covered cooking shelter complete with a wood stove. **Sundre Visitor Information Centre** (403/638-3245, summer daily 10 A.M.–6 P.M.) is on the east bank of the Red Deer River.

Caroline

Named after the daughter of one of the town's earliest settlers, Caroline is the hometown of four-time World Men's Figure Skating champion **Kurt Browning.** His portrait adorns local tourist literature, and the town's Kurt Browning Arena (48th Ave., Mon.–Fri. 8 A.M.–4 P.M.) houses Kurt's Korner, a display of personal memorabilia.

ROCKY MOUNTAIN HOUSE

Best known simply as "Rocky," this town of 6,800 straddles the North Saskatchewan River and is surrounded by gently rolling hills in a transition zone between aspen parkland and mountains. Highway 11 (also known as David Thompson Highway) passes through town on its way east to Red Deer (82 km/51 mi) and west to the northern end of Banff National Park (170 km/106 mi).

Rocky Mountain House National Historic Site

This National Historic Site (seven km/4.3 mi west of Rocky Mountain House on Hwy. 11A, 403/845-2412, mid-May–Aug. daily 10 A.M.–5 P.M., Sept. Mon.–Fri. 10 A.M.–5 P.M.,

adult $4, senior $3.50, child $2) commemorates the important role fur trading played in Canada's history. The first trading post, or fort, was built on the site in 1799. By the 1830s, beaver felt was out of fashion in Europe, and traders turned to buffalo robes. By the 1870s, the fur trade had ended and the last post at Rocky Mountain House closed. Today, the protected areas include the sites of five forts, a buffalo paddock, and a stretch of riverbank where the large voyageur canoes would have come ashore to be loaded with furs bound for Europe. The visitor center is the best place to begin a visit to the site; its interpretive displays detail the history of the forts, the fur trade, and exploration of the West. Two trails lead along the north bank of the river. The longer of the two, a 3.2-kilometer (two-mile) loop, passes the site of the two original forts. Frequent "listening posts" along the trail play a lively recorded commentary on life in the early 1800s. All that remains of the forts are depressions in the ground, but

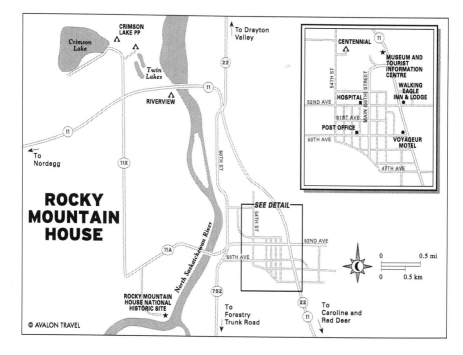

through the commentary and interpretive displays, it is easy to get a good idea of what the forts looked like.

Rocky Mountain House Museum

Rocky Mountain House Museum (5406 48th St., 403/845-2332, July–Aug. daily 9 A.M.–8 P.M., June and Sept. daily 9 A.M.–5 P.M., the rest of the year weekdays only, adult $4, child $1.50) is in the same complex as the information center. Exhibits include an array of pioneer artifacts, including an early Forest Service cabin, a one-room schoolhouse, and an interesting rope-making machine.

Accommodations and Camping

Least expensive of the motels spread out along Highway 11 east of town is the **Voyageur Motel** (403/845-3381 or 888/845-5569, www. voyageurmotel.ca, $60–75's, $75–90 d), which has large clean rooms with fridge and microwave, or pay an extra $15 for a kitchenette. **Walking Eagle Inn & Lodge** (4819 45th St., 403/845-2804 or 866/845-2131, www.walkingeagle.net, $99–129 s or d), easily recognized by its striking log exterior, has comfortable rooms, a steakhouse restaurant, and a steam room.

Riverview Campground (Hwy. 11, 403/845-4422, unserviced sites $16, hookups $19–26) is the only commercial camping facility in town. The unserviced sites are tucked in among a grove of trees along the North Saskatchewan River. Amenities include a small grocery store, laundry, showers, and free firewood. Another recommended spot is **◖ Crimson Lake Provincial Park** (403/845-2330, $22–28), northwest of town along an access road off Highway 11, where you'll find two campgrounds; sites along the bank of Crimson Lake are mostly powered, whereas those beside Twin Lakes aren't.

Information

Make your first stop in town the tourist information center (54th Ave., 403/845-5450 or 800/565-3793, www.rockychamber.org, late May–Aug. Mon.–Sat. 9 A.M.–7 P.M., Sun. 10 A.M.–6 P.M., the rest of the year Mon.–Fri. 9 A.M.–5 P.M.), beside Highway 11 north of downtown.

DAVID THOMPSON HIGHWAY

The David Thompson Highway (Hwy. 11) climbs slowly from the aspen parkland around Rocky Mountain House westward into the dense forests on the eastern slopes of the Canadian Rockies.

Nordegg

The only community between Rocky and Banff National Park is Nordegg (population 100), 85 kilometers (53 miles) west of Rocky. Established in 1914, Nordegg was a "planned" coal-mining town. The streets were built in a semicircular pattern, centered around the railroad station and shops. Fifty miners' cottages were built, all painted in pastel colors. Gardens were planted, two churches and a hospital were built, and a golf course was developed—miners had never had it better. But the mine closed in early 1955, and by summer it had been abandoned.

The original townsite has mostly disappeared, but remaining mine structures are preserved as a National Historic Site. The Nordegg Historical Society, made up of many former residents, operates the **Nordegg Heritage Centre** (403/721-2625, mid-May–Sept. daily 9 A.M.–5 P.M., free) in a two-story former school building along the main street. Also in this building is the **Miner's Café**, where the soup and sandwich special is $8, and the sandwiches are stacked and delicious. Freshly made fruit pies are an easy choice for dessert. Uphill (within walking distance) from the museum complex is the original townsite, now with only a few buildings still standing. Visitors are free to wander around at their leisure, but ask at the heritage center for a map. Continuing up the hill is the mine infrastructure, much of which still remains. The only access to this section of Nordegg is on a guided tour. These depart twice daily through summer, and are booked through the heritage center. Neither tour goes underground, but the longer version ($8) takes in the briquette processing plants and mine entrances. Call ahead for a schedule.

A good option for budget travelers is **HI-Nordegg** (403/721-2140, www.hihostels.ca, dorms $24–28, $65.50–73.50 s or d), also known as Shunda Creek Hostel. Affiliated with Hostelling International, this huge log chalet in a wilderness setting has a fully equipped kitchen, dining room, fireplace, hot showers, and an outdoor hot tub.

West from Nordegg

Twenty-three kilometers (14 miles) west of Nordegg, an unpaved side road leads eight kilometers (five miles) north to **Crescent Falls,** where there is primitive camping. Back on the highway, the brilliant turquoise water of **Abraham Lake,** one of Alberta's largest reservoirs, comes into view. Don't stop for a photo session just yet, though, because the views improve farther west. **◖ Aurum Lodge** (45 km/28 mi west of Nordegg, 40 km/25 mi east of the Banff National Park, 403/721-2117, www.aurumlodge.com, $149–199 s, $179–229 d, self-contained units $189–249) trades on an eco-friendly stance and wonderfully scenic location overlooking Abraham Lake. Owners Alan and Madeleine Ernst used recycled materials wherever possible during construction, natural light streams into all corners, the kitchen uses a wood-fired stove, and much of the waste is recycled. But don't imagine some backwoods cabin without running water—it's a comfortable and modern lodge. Rooms in the main lodge are simply decorated, but bright and immaculately kept. Cozy self-contained cottages offer a bathroom, kitchen with woodstove, and lots of privacy. **David Thompson Resort** (403/721-2103 or 888/810-2103, www.davidthompsonresort.com, May–mid-Oct., unserviced sites $21, hookups $31–38, motel rooms and cabins $101 s or d) provides a variety of lodging options. The bathroom facilities were in need of an upgrade at the time of our research trip for this edition, but as a trade off there's a unique open-sided bar that opens for karaoke each night and then again in the morning for a pancake breakfast. Other facilities include a playground with massive slides, Frisbee-golf course, restaurant, and gas station.

At the south end of Abraham Lake, **Kootenay Plains Ecological Reserve** protects a unique area of dry grasslands in the mountains. The climate in this section of the valley is unusually moderate, making it a prime wintering area for elk, mule deer, bighorn sheep, and moose. For thousands of years, the Kootenay peoples would cross the mountains from the Columbia River Valley to hunt these mammals and the bison that were then prolific. Because of the dry microclimate and its associated vegetation, mammals are not abundant in summer.

Two designated wilderness areas near the west end of Highway 11—**White Goat** and **Siffleur**—afford experienced hikers the chance to enjoy the natural beauty and wildlife of the Canadian Rockies away from the crowds associated with the mountain national parks. Both are protected from any activities that could have an impact on the area's fragile ecosystems, including road and trail development. No bridges have been built over the area's many fast-flowing streams, and the few old trails that do exist are not maintained. The only access to these parks is on foot, meaning they are lightly traveled. The main trail into Siffleur Wilderness Area begins from a parking area two kilometers (1.2 miles) south of the Two O'Clock Creek Campground at Kootenay Plains; it's worth mentioning for photogenic **Siffleur Falls,** four kilometers (2.5 miles) from the highway. For more information contact the **Department of Tourism, Parks and Recreation** (403/845-8349, www.albertaparks.ca).

CALGARY TO RED DEER

The original road (Hwy. 2A) between Calgary and Edmonton is now bypassed entirely by Highway 2, a four-lane divided road that makes the trip an easy three-hour drive, with Red Deer marking the midway point.

Carstairs

Carstairs is a small farming, dairy, and ranching

center 67 kilometers (42 miles) north of Calgary. The town's tree-lined streets are dotted with grand old houses, and the grain elevators associated with all prairie towns stand silhouetted against the skyline. The official attractions are outside of town, including **PaSu Farm** (10 km/6.2 mi west of town, 403/337-2800, Tues.–Sat. 10 A.M.–4 P.M., Sun. noon–4 P.M.), a working farm with a dozen breeds of sheep. It also displays a wide variety of sheepskin and wool products, as well as weavings from Africa. The farm's restaurant serves light lunches plus scones, homemade apple pie, and various teas Tuesday–Saturday noon–4 P.M., along with a Sunday lunch (noon–2:30 P.M.). Much of the wool from PaSu Farm is sold to **Custom Woolen Mills** (403/337-2221, Mon.–Fri. 9 A.M.–3 P.M.), on the other side of Carstairs, 20 kilometers (12.5 miles) east on Highway 581 and 4.5 kilometers (2.8 miles) north on Highway 791. At this working museum, the raw wool is processed on clunky-looking machines—some of which date to the 1880s—into wools and yarns ready for knitting (and sale). A self-guided tour is offered.

Olds and Vicinity

Olds is a little more than halfway between Calgary and Red Deer. Surrounded by rich farmland, it's the home of **Olds College** (403/556-8281), which has been a leader in the development of Canadian agriculture for the last 100 years. Visitors are free to wander around the campus, admiring colorful beds of well-tended, prairie-hardy plants. The 600-hectare (1,480-acre) campus is along Highway 2, south of the main street.

Red Lodge Provincial Park protects a forested stretch of the Little Red Deer River 28 kilometers (17.5 miles) northwest of Olds. The park is situated within an ideal habitat for deer and moose. The campground (403/224-2547, mid-Apr.–mid-Oct., $22–28) has a kitchen shelter, coin-operated showers, and firewood, and the river is good for swimming, floating, and fishing.

Torrington

Torrington, on Highway 27, 28 kilometers (17.5 miles) east of Olds, has more gophers than residents. This wouldn't be unusual for a prairie town, except that Torrington's gophers are all stuffed. The **Gopher Hole Museum** (208 1st St., 403/631-3931, June–Sept. daily 10 A.M.–5 P.M., $2.50) is described as "a whimsical portrayal of daily life in our tranquil village." And that it is—approximately 40 dioramas house stuffed gophers in various poses, including gophers in love, gophers playing sports, trailer-court gophers, and even gophers wearing shirts declaring that animal rights activists, who were incensed at the idea of the museum, should "Go stuff themselves." Admission includes a copy of the words to the *Torrington Gopher Call Song,* which wafts through the quiet streets of the village whenever the museum is open.

Dry Island Buffalo Jump

This 1,180-hectare (2,900-acre) park is named for both an isolated mesa in the Red Deer River Valley and the site where natives stampeded bison over a cliff approximately 2,000 years ago. The buffalo jump—a 50-meter (164-foot) drop—is much higher than other jumps in Alberta and is in an ideal location; the approach to the jump is uphill, masking the presence of a cliff until the final few meters. Below the prairie benchland, cliff-like valley walls and banks of sandstone have been carved into strange-looking badlands by wind and water erosion. A great diversity of plantlife grows in the valley; more than 400 species of flowering plants have been recorded. The park is a day-use area only; apart from a picnic area and a few trails, it is undeveloped. Access is along a gravel road east from Highway 21. From the park entrance, at the top of the buffalo jump, the road descends steeply for 200 vertical meters (660 feet) into the valley (it can be extremely slippery after rain) to the bank of the Red Deer River.

Innisfail

Innisfail Historical Village (in the fairgrounds at 42nd St. and 52nd Ave., 403/227-2906, summer Mon.–Sat. 10 A.M.–5 P.M., Sun.

noon–5 P.M., donation) has re-created historic buildings, including a stopping house, a school, a store, a Canadian Pacific Railway (C.P.R.) station, and a blacksmith's shop, on a one-hectare (1.5-acre) site. The Royal Canadian Mounted Police (RCMP) **Police Dog Service Training Centre** (four km/2.5 mi south of town, 403/227-3346, free) is where police dog handlers and their four-legged companions come from across Canada to receive training in obedience, agility, and criminal apprehension. Through summer, public demonstrations are given every Wednesday at 2 P.M. Bookings are not required, but the small grandstand is usually full by start time, so arrive early for the best seats.

Markerville

This town, 16 kilometers (10 miles) west then three kilometers (1.9 miles) north of Innisfail, was originally settled by Icelandic people in the 1880s, who had settled in eastern Canada but after finding the land unproductive continued west. Today, around 100 people—most of

Markerville is one of Alberta's most attractive towns.

whom trace their heritage back to the original settlers—call Markerville home. It's a pretty village, with smartly painted homes and well-kept gardens. The only official attraction is **Markerville Creamery** (403/728-3006, mid-May–early Sept. Mon.–Sat. 10 A.M.–5:30 P.M., Sun. noon–5:30 P.M.). Between 1902 and the time of its closure in 1972, the creamery won many awards for its fine-quality butters, as you'll learn on a self-guided tour ($2) of the butter-making process. Part of the creamery has been converted to a *kaffistofa* (café) with a choice of Icelandic specialties.

The most famous of the Icelandic immigrants was Stephan A. Stephansson, one of the Western world's most prolific poets. He spent the early part of his life in his homeland, but most of his poetry was written in Canada. Just north of Markerville is his restored 1927 home, the distinctive pink-and-green colored **Stephansson House** (403/728-3929, mid-May–Aug. daily 10 A.M.–6 P.M., adult $3, senior and child $2). Interpretive panels beside the parking lot tell the story of Stephansson and his fellow immigrants, while a short trail leads through a grove of trees to the house itself.

RED DEER

This city of 86,000 (Alberta's third-largest) is on a bend of the Red Deer River, halfway between the cities of Calgary and Edmonton, which are 145 kilometers (90 miles) south and 148 kilometers (92 miles) north, respectively. From the highway, Red Deer seems to be all industrial estates and suburban sprawl, but an extensive park system runs through the city, and many historic buildings have been restored.

The name Red Deer was mentioned on maps by explorer David Thompson in the early 1800s. The Cree name for the river is *Waskasoo* (elk); scholars believe that Thompson translated the word incorrectly, confusing these animals with the red deer of Scotland.

Sights

If you're arriving in Red Deer from either the north or south, stay on Highway 2 until the

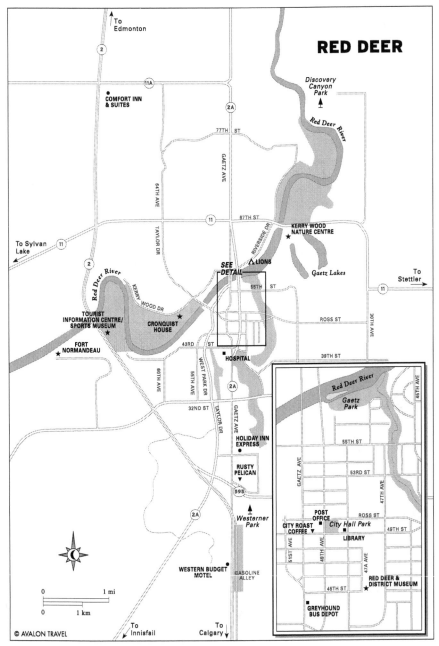

RED DEER

To Edmonton

Discovery Canyon Park

Red Deer River

COMFORT INN & SUITES

77TH ST

GAETZ AVE

64TH AVE

TAYLOR DR

11

87TH ST

RIVERSIDE DR

KERRY WOOD NATURE CENTRE

To Sylvan Lake

Red Deer River

KERRY WOOD DR

LIONS

55TH ST

Gaetz Lakes

To Stettler

ROSS ST

130TH AVE

TOURIST INFORMATION CENTRE/ SPORTS MUSEUM

CRONQUIST HOUSE

FORT NORMANDEAU

43RD ST

39TH ST

WEST PARK DR

60TH AVE

55TH AVE

TAYLOR DR

GAETZ AVE

HOSPITAL

32ND ST

HOLIDAY INN EXPRESS

RUSTY PELICAN

595

Westerner Park

WESTERN BUDGET MOTEL

GASOLINE ALLEY

0   1 mi
0   1 km

© AVALON TRAVEL

To Innisfail

To Calgary

Detail inset

Red Deer River

Gaetz Park

46TH AVE

55TH ST

GAETZ AVE

53RD ST

47TH AVE

POST OFFICE

ROSS ST

CITY ROAST COFFEE

City Hall Park

49TH ST

51ST AVE

49TH AVE

47A AVE

LIBRARY

46TH ST

RED DEER & DISTRICT MUSEUM

GREYHOUND BUS DEPOT

large red-and-white **Red Deer Visitor and Convention Bureau** building comes into view (from the north, take the 32nd St. exit and loop back onto Hwy. 2 northbound). In addition to being a good source of information, it is home to the **Alberta Sports Hall of Fame and Museum** (Hwy. 2, in the same building as the Red Deer Visitor and Convention Bureau, 403/341-8614, summer daily 9 A.M.–6 P.M., the rest of the year daily 10 A.M.–5 P.M., adult $3, child $2). Displays highlight the feats of Albertan sporting heroes such as hockey legend Wayne Gretzky, multiple-time World Figure Skating Champion Kurt Browning, and Red Deer girl Jamie Sale, who, with partner David Pelletier, was belatedly awarded a skating gold medal at the 2002 Winter Olympics after the infamous judging controversy. But it's not all about winter sports—you can also admire the achievements of Albertans like Sharon Wood (the first North American woman to summit Mount Everest) and Jason Zuback (multiple world long drive golfing champion). From this point, it's possible to walk (or drive via 32nd St.) to **Fort Normandeau** (403/346-2010, mid-May–June daily noon–5 P.M., July–Aug. daily noon–8 P.M., free). This replica is built on the site of a fort constructed in the spring of 1885 in anticipation of the Riel Rebellion—a Métis uprising led by Louis Riel.

The downtown **Red Deer and District Museum** (4525 47A Ave., 403/309-8405, July and Aug. Mon.–Fri. 10 A.M.–5 P.M. and Sat.–Sun. 1–5 P.M., the rest of the year daily noon–5 P.M., donation), which reopened in early 2010 after extensive renovations, tells the story of the area from prehistoric times to the present, with emphasis on the growth and development of the last 100 years. If you have youngsters in tow, head for interactive Children's Zone; if you have a love of the tacky and wacky, search out the display of The World's Most Boring Postcard, a title bestowed on a postcard depicting the museum exterior.

A DAY AT THE BEACH

Landlocked Albertans don't have a great deal of choice when it comes to a vacation on the beach, unless they head over the mountains to Invermere, in British Columbia, or jump aboard an airplane. One of the exceptions is **Sylvan Lake,** 22 kilometers (14 miles) west of Red Deer, which has been a popular summer resort since the beginning of the 20th century. It has more than five kilometers (three miles) of sandy beaches, clean warm water, a large marina, and plenty of recreation facilities. Kids will love **Wild Rapids** (Lakeshore Dr., 403/887-3636) and its 11 water slides, heated pool, and sailboard and paddleboat rentals. The beachy stretch of lake is lined with surf-clothing shops, water-sport rentals, casual cafés, kid-friendly accommodations, and even a lighthouse. In the vicinity, Gull, Pigeon, and Miquelon Lakes have pleasant beaches and warm water for swimming.

Recreation

Straddling the Red Deer River is 11-kilometer-long (seven-mile-long) **Waskasoo Park.** The park has a 75-kilometer (47-mile) trail system, which is good for walking or biking in summer and cross-country skiing in winter. If you've stopped at the highway-side information center, it's possible to drive through the one-way gate to adjacent **Heritage Ranch** (403/347-4977), where trail rides are $35 per hour.

Continuing downstream, **Kerry Wood Nature Centre** (6300 45th Ave., 403/346-2010, daily 10 A.M.–5 P.M.) has various exhibits and videos on the natural history of the river valley and provides access to a paved walking trail through the adjacent 118-hectare (292-acre) **Gaetz Lakes Sanctuary.** Protected since 1924, this parkland of spruce and poplar interspersed with marshes is home to 128 recorded species of birds and 25 species of mammals.

Children will love **Discovery Canyon Park** (403/343-8311, daily 9 A.M.–8 P.M. in summer), which is all about discovering fun rather than learning. The highlight is a natural stream that has been modified into a waterslide, complete with rapids and a big pool at one end. Admission is free and tube rental is $3. To get there, follow 30th Ave, four kilometers (2.5 miles) north of 67th Street.

Accommodations and Camping

Red Deer's location between Alberta's two largest cities makes it a popular location for conventions and conferences, so the city has a lot of hotels. The cheapies are at the south end of the city along "Gasoline Alley." Try **Western Budget Motel** (37468 Hwy. 2 S, 403/358-5755, www.westernbudgetmotel.com, $59–99 s, $79–99 d), on the western side of Gasoline Alley, where the rooms are the best value between Calgary and Edmonton—they are clean, spacious, and relatively modern.

The **Holiday Inn Express** is south of downtown on the northbound side of the road (2803 Gaetz Ave., 403/343-2112 or 877/660-8550, www.hiexpress.com, $119–169 s or d). The rooms are spacious, modern, and well furnished. Breakfast is included in the rates, as is access to an indoor saltwater pool.

While the Western Budget Motel provides excellent value, my pick of the Red Deer accommodations insofar as room quality goes is the **C Comfort Inn & Suites** (6846 66th St., 403/348-0025 or 866/348-0025, www.comfortinnreddeer.com, $140 s or d), just off Highway 2 at the north end of town. Opened in 2005, the spacious rooms are filled with modern conveniences, a light breakfast is included in the rates, and there's an indoor pool with a waterslide. Another reason to stay is this motel's eco-friendly design, which includes a roof covered in solar power panels.

Red Deer has good city camping at the treed **Lions Campground,** on the west side of the river (4759 Riverside Dr., 403/342-8183, May–Sept., unserviced sites $19, powered sites $29). To get there, follow Gaetz Avenue north through town and turn right after crossing the Red Deer River. The campground has showers, full hookups, and a laundry room.

Food

Head to **City Roast Coffee** (4940 Ross St.,

403/347-0893, Mon.–Sat. 7:30 A.M.–6 P.M.) for a caffeine fix in a city-style coffeehouse. Around the corner, a very different type of eatery, the **Jerry Can** (5005 50th Ave., 403/347-9417, open daily for breakfast and lunch), attracts a strange collection of locals who come for the inexpensive meals and to catch up on gossip.

Fast-food and family-style restaurants line 50th (Gaetz) Avenue north and south of downtown, but for Red Deer's most distinguished dining experience plan on eating at the **C Rusty Pelican** (2079 50th Ave., 403/347-1414, daily 11 A.M.–10 P.M., $14–29). Mains range from the semi-exotic (Cajun-style red snapper) to the traditional (prime rib of beef with Yorkshire pudding). A menu filled with seafood starters, a sensibly priced wine list, and melt-in-your-mouth strawberry cheesecake round out this top pick.

Information and Services

The Red Deer Visitor and Convention Bureau operates the excellent tourist information center (403/346-0180 or 800/215-8946, www.tourismreddeer.net, year-round Mon.–Fri. 9 A.M.–5 P.M., Sat.–Sun. 10 A.M.–5 P.M., until 6 P.M. in summer) on Highway 2 between the main north and south entrances to the city. It's on the city side of the highway (if you're arriving from the north, take the 32nd St. exit and loop back onto Hwy. 2 northbound). In addition to providing a load of information, the center has a gift shop, a concession area, and restrooms, and is adjacent to a picnic area.

Red Deer Public Library is an excellent facility housed in a single-story, red-brick building behind City Hall (4818 49th St., 403/346-4576, Mon.–Thurs. 9:30 A.M.–8:30 P.M., Fri.–Sat. 9:30 A.M.–5:30 P.M., Sun. 1:30–5 P.M.).

Getting There

Two scheduled bus services link Red Deer to Calgary and Edmonton. **Greyhound** departs from the depot (4303 Gaetz Ave., 403/343-8866) throughout the day for both cities. **Red Arrow** (403/531-0350 or 800/232-1958, www.

redarrow.ca) offers a more luxurious service, with complimentary beverages and snacks. Their buses depart north of downtown at 5315 54th Street four times daily for Calgary and Edmonton.

LACOMBE

From Red Deer, Highway 2 continues 30 kilometers (19 miles) north to Lacombe, a town of 9,000 that centers on a main street lined with Edwardian-era buildings.

Big-hitting golfers should consider a stop at the nearby **Nursery Golf & Country Club** (Range Rd. 27–0, 403/782-5400, greens fees $42), which is home to Canada's longest golf hole. It's the 11th hole, a par 6 stretching to 782 yards from the back markers. Turn off Highway 2 four kilometers (2.5 miles) north of town.

◖ Lacombe Corn Maze

Only open when the corn reaches a height of six feet, the Lacombe Corn Maze (Hwy. 12, 403/782-4653, late July–Aug. Mon.–Sat. 11 A.M.–9 P.M., Sept.–mid-Oct. Wed.–Fri. 4–8 P.M., Sat. 11 A.M.–8 P.M., adult $9, child

© ANDREW HEMPSTEAD

The Lacombe Corn Maze changes design each year.

$7) is a rural highlight of central Alberta, even for adults. Cut in a different design each year, it takes at least an hour to get through, with a "cheat sheet" for those who get truly lost. Also on site is a petting zoo, a tire horse carousel, a corn cannon, a jumping pillow, and miniature train rides to keep the young ones amused for a bit longer.

Practicalities

Between Highway 2 and downtown is a campground and an information center (www.lacombetourism.com), but for motel accommodations, stay on the highway to reach **Wolf Creek Inn** (Hwy. 2, 403/782-4716, $70 s or d). Overlooking a small lake, it's home to 20 simple rooms and has a restaurant that is a popular spot for highway travelers looking to avoid fast-food joints. Access is only from Highway 2 southbound, so if you're heading toward Edmonton, take the second exit and loop back south via the overpass.

HIGHWAY 12 EAST

From Lacombe, it's 70 kilometers (43 miles) west to Stettler on Highway 12. Out of sight to the north is **Buffalo Lake,** a large, shallow body of water surrounded by a hummocky area created by receding ice during the last Ice Age. On the lake's southern shore is ◖ **Ol' MacDonalds Resort** (off Hwy. 835, 403/742-6603, www.olmacdonalds.com, May–Sept., unserviced $25–28, hookups $32–40, cabins $62–150 s or d), a sprawling campground offering over 300 treed sites and an amazing array of things to do. Aside from the beach with shallow, warm water, there's watercraft rentals, evening wagon rides, a petting zoo, indoor mini-golf within a museum, an antique carousel, a café, and bike and buggy rentals.

Stettler

The farming town of Stettler (population 5,800) is home to **Alberta Prairie Railway Excursions** (403/742-2811, www.ab-steamtrain.com), a tourist train that runs south to the even smaller town of Big Valley. A rollicking good time is had by all, with live music, the occasional train robbery, and a hearty meal served at the turnaround point. Check the website for a schedule; the train runs each weekend May through October (and Thurs. and Fri. in July and Aug.). The fare is adult $85, youth $65, child $35. Stettler also offers the **Town and Country Museum** (6302 44th Ave., 403/742-4534, May–early Sept. daily 10 A.M.–5:30 P.M., adult $3, senior and child $2), a surprisingly large complex comprising over two dozen buildings spread over three hectares (7.5 acres). Highlights include the imposing courthouse, a railway station, and a small farmhouse that provided a home for three generations of the same family.

The nicest of five accommodations in town is **Ramada Inn & Suites** (6711 49th Ave., at the west entrance to town, 403/742-6555 or 888/442-6555, www.ramada.com, $145 s or d), a solid four-story chain hotel that opened in 2007. **Town of Stettler Campground** (6202 44th Ave., 403/742-4411, May–Oct., $14–20) is across the road from a spray park on the west side of town.

Big Knife Provincial Park

Legend has it that Big Knife Creek was named after a fight between two long-standing enemies—one Cree, the other Blackfoot—that resulted in the death of both men. The park's small campground (mid-May–mid-Sept., $18) has limited facilities, but the Battle River flows through the park, making for good swimming and canoeing. To get to the park from Stettler, head east along Highway 12 approximately 40 kilometers (25 miles) to Halkirk, then north on Highway 855 another 20 kilometers (12.5 miles).

Gooseberry Lake Provincial Park

This small park, 14 kilometers (8.7 miles) north of Consort, is on the shore of a tree-encircled lake and is made up of rolling grassland and a series of alkaline ponds. Many birds, including the northern phalarope, use the lake as a staging area along their migratory paths. The campground (403/742-7512, mid-May–mid-Sept., $20–25) is between the lake and a

nine-hole golf course and has a kitchen shelter and firewood.

WETASKIWIN

This town, halfway between Red Deer and Edmonton on Highway 2A, is an important wheat-farming and cattle-ranching center of 11,000. In the language of the Cree, Wetaskiwin ("Where Peace was Made") is a reference to nearby hills where a treaty between the Cree and Blackfoot was signed in 1867.

Reynolds-Alberta Museum

This world-class facility, two kilometers (1.2 miles) west of downtown (Hwy. 13, 780/361-1351, daily 10 A.M.–5 P.M., closed Mon. Sept.–May, adult $9, senior $7, child $5), does a wonderful job of cataloging the history of transportation in Alberta, from horse-drawn carriages to luxurious 1950s automobiles. Over 1,000 vehicles have been fully restored, but some, such as a handmade snowmobile, are in their original condition. At the far end of the main room, you can peer into a large hall where the restoration takes place. The transportation displays encircle a large area where traditional farm machinery is on show, from the most basic plow to a massive combine harvester.

Behind the museum lies an airstrip and a large hangar that houses **Canada's Aviation Hall of Fame.** The Hall of Fame recognizes those who have made contributions to the history of aviation and contains several vintage aircraft. Admission is included with a ticket to the Reynolds-Alberta Museum. Hours are also the same. Operating out of the Hall of Fame, **Central Aviation** (780/352-9689) offers a 10-minute flight in an old biplane for $119; weekends only.

Accommodations and Food

Looking for a regular motel room? Try the **Super 8 Motel** (3820 56th St., 780/361-3808 or 800/800-8000, www.super8.com, $109–119 s or d), a newer place that is within walking distance of the museum. Rates include continental breakfast. Opposite the local golf course, **Wetaskiwin Lions RV Campground**

(2.5 km/1.6 mi east of town along Hwy. 13, 780/352-7258, May–Sept., unserviced sites $18, hookups $24–26) has free showers, an Internet kiosk, a laundry room, a cooking shelter, a stocked trout pond, and mini-golf.

Grandma Lee's Bakery (5103 50th Ave., 780/352-7711, Mon.–Sat. 7:30 A.M.–5 P.M.) is enduringly popular with locals for its small-town atmosphere as much as its food. Recommended are the meat pies and tasty pastries. A few doors away, the **Stanley Café** (5015 50th Ave., 780/352-3633, daily noon–8 P.M., $7–11.50) is a plain diner with Westernized Chinese food at low prices. Opposite the information center is **Runway Lunch** (5505 50th Ave., 780/352-3777, Mon.–Fri. 7:30 A.M.–4 P.M., lunches $5.50–8), where the home-style cooking is a welcome respite from the blandness of the fast-food joints lining nearby 56th Street.

Information

At the junction of Highway 2A and 50th Avenue, the local **tourist information center** (4910 55th St., 780/352-8003, year-round Mon.–Fri. 9 A.M.–5 P.M., as well as summer weekends 9 A.M.–3 P.M.) is impossible to miss—just look for the colorful water tower across the road.

CAMROSE AND VICINITY

The population of Camrose, 40 kilometers (25 miles) east of Wetaskiwin, swells the first weekend of August when country music fans descend on the local exhibition grounds for the **Big Valley Jamboree** (780/672-0224 or 888/404-1234, www.bigvalleyjamboree.com), one of North America's largest such gatherings. Daily passes are around $80, and a three-day weekend pass goes for $195; camping is $120 for as long as you can handle the heat, the noise, and the booze (actually, it's not that bad—a great time is had by all).

As a tribute to early Norwegian settlers, a nine-meter (30-foot) scaled-down replica of a Viking longship is on display in the **Bill Fowler Centre** (5402 48th Ave., 780/672-4217, summer Mon.–Fri. 8:30 A.M.–8 P.M. and Sat.–Sun.

9:30 A.M.–5:30 P.M., the rest of the year Mon.–Fri. 8:30 A.M.–4:30 P.M., free). Overlooking Mirror Lake, this building is also home to the local **tourist information center** and the start of a 10-kilometer (6.2-mile) trail system that encircles the lake (2.2 km/1.4 mi) and follows Camrose Creek south to the campground.

Accommodations and Food

Just a couple of blocks from Mirror Lake, the centrally located **Camrose Motel** (6116 48th Ave., 780/672-3364, from $70 s or d) has 20 basic rooms, each with a microwave and a small fridge. The town-operated **Valleyview Campground** (5204 50th Ave., May–Sept., $15–20) has powered sites, showers, a kitchen shelter, and firewood. To get there, follow 53rd Street south from Highway 13 for two kilometers (1.2 miles) and turn left on 39th Avenue.

The friendly, country-style atmosphere is similar at **Camrose Railway Station** (44th St., 780/672-3099, mid-May–Aug. Thurs.–Fri. 1–5 P.M., Sat. 10 A.M.–5 P.M.). It's typical tearoom fare in a restored station. Call ahead for a Saturday schedule—often it's a theme with links to Camrose's past (German, Ukrainian, Native, etc).

Along the highway through town, the **Monte Carlo Restaurant** (4907 48th Ave., Sun.–Mon. 11 A.M.–8 P.M., Tues.–Thurs. 11 A.M.–9 P.M., Fri.–Sat. 11 A.M.–10 P.M., $14–26) is the most popular place in town for a special night out, although the menu isn't particularly creative (think fettuccini alfredo, roast chicken, fish-and-chips, and pork souvlaki).

Miquelon Lake Provincial Park

This 906-hectare (2,240-acre) park, 30 kilometers (19 miles) north of Camrose on Highway 833, is part of the massive 650-square-kilometer (250-square-mile) **Cooking Lake Moraine**, a hummocky, forested region dotted with lakes that extends north to Elk Island National Park. At the end of the last Ice Age, as the sheet of ice that covered much of the continent receded, it occasionally stalled, as it did in this area. Chunks of ice then broke off and melted, depositing glacial till in mounds. Between the mounds are hollows, known as kettles, which have filled with water. The **Knob and Kettle Trail System** starts behind the baseball diamond and is a series of short interconnecting trails through this intriguing landscape. The draw for most visitors is the wide beach fronting a warm and shallow bay. Other amenities include a modern visitor center, a large playground, and an adjacent golf course (780/672-7308). The ◖ **park campground** (780/672-7274, unserviced sites $22, powered sites $28) has modern washrooms, kitchen shelters, and firewood.

East on Highway 14

From Miquelon Lake Provincial Park it's a short drive north to **Tofield,** from where Highway 14 heads 180 kilometers (112 miles) southeast to Wainwright and then continues east into Saskatchewan. East of Tofield is **Beaverhill Natural Area,** western Canada's only shorebird reserve. The protected area centers on a large, shallow lake where more than 250 bird species have been recorded. **Beaverhill Lake Nature Centre** (403/662-3191, summer Tues.–Sat. 10 A.M.–6 P.M., Sun. 2–4 P.M., free) is an interpretive center with maps of the area and bird checklists. Campers gravitate to **Lindbrook Star Gazer Campground** (51123 Range Rd. 200, 780/662-4439, www.lindbrookstargazer.ca, late May–Sept., $32–37), which has an outdoor swimming pool. To get there from Tofield, head 10 kilometers (6.2 miles) west on Highway 14 then three kilometers (1.9 miles) north on SH 630.

Southeast of **Viking** are two "rib stones," carved with a design resembling bison ribs that have been dated at 1,000 years old. The stones held special significance for generations of Plains Indians, whose lives revolved around the movement of bison herds. They believed that by conducting certain ceremonial rites and

by leaving gifts of beads or tobacco around the stones, their luck in hunting would improve. They then gave thanks by leaving more gifts after a successful hunt. The site is not well marked. Fourteen kilometers (8.7 miles) east of Viking on Highway 14 is a historical marker. A little farther east is a gravel road to the south; follow this road two kilometers (1.2 miles) to Highway 615, turn east (left), then take the first gravel road to the south (right) and follow it for 2.5 kilometers (1.5 miles) to a low knoll surrounded by fields. A provincial historic cairn marks the site.

The last town along Highway 14 before Saskatchewan, Wainwright is best known for the military's 400-square-kilometer (154 square miles) **CFB/ASU Wainwright,** a training facility used mostly by reservists. A small head of bison (turn left at the guarded entrance, then right down the fence line for best viewing opportunities) is the only reminder of a national park created in 1908 to protect plains bison. A local restaurant, the ◖ **Honey Pot Eatery & Pub** (823 2nd Ave., 780/842-4094, Mon.–Sat. 11 A.M.–9:30 P.M., Sun. 11 A.M.–2 P.M., $12–20), is worthy of a mention for the fact that it has been serving up healthy food for much longer than it has been trendy. It's been open since 1979, serving hungry locals and travelers alike dishes as varied as grilled arctic char and elk smothered in saskatoon berries.

Dillberry Lake Provincial Park is on the Alberta/Saskatchewan border, 50 kilometers (31 miles) southeast of Wainwright. The lake is surrounded by sandy beaches and low sand dunes (the biggest dunes are at the southeastern end of the lake), and its clear spring-fed waters are good for swimming. A 200-site campground (780/858-3824, mid-May–mid-Sept., unserviced sites $20, powered sites $26) is behind the park's finest beach and has showers, kitchen shelters, and firewood.

www.moon.com

DESTINATIONS | ACTIVITIES | BLOGS | MAPS | BOOKS

MOON.COM is ready to help plan your next trip! Filled with fresh trip ideas and strategies, author interviews, informative travel blogs, a detailed map library, and descriptions of all the Moon guidebooks, Moon.com is all you need to get out and explore the world—or even places in your own backyard. While at Moon.com, sign up for our monthly e-newsletter for updates on new releases, travel tips, and expert advice from our on-the-go Moon authors. As always, when you travel with Moon, expect an experience that is uncommon and truly unique.

MOON IS ON FACEBOOK—BECOME A FAN!
JOIN THE MOON PHOTO GROUP ON FLICKR

MAP SYMBOLS

▦▦▦	Expressway	**〖**	Highlight	✗	Airfield	⚓	Golf Course
——	Primary Road	○	City/Town	✈	Airport	▣	Parking Area
▦▦▦	Secondary Road	◉	State Capital	▲	Mountain	▰	Archaeological Site
▫▫▫	Unpaved Road	✹	National Capital	✚	Unique Natural Feature	⬩	Church
- - - -	Trail	·★	Point of Interest			⬛	Gas Station
·········	Ferry	•	Accommodation	⬎	Waterfall	◌	Glacier
━·━·━	Railroad	▼	Restaurant/Bar	▲	Park	⬚	Mangrove
▦▦▦	Pedestrian Walkway	■	Other Location	⬛	Trailhead	▨	Reef
▥▥▥	Stairs	Λ	Campground	⚶	Skiing Area	▱	Swamp

CONVERSION TABLES

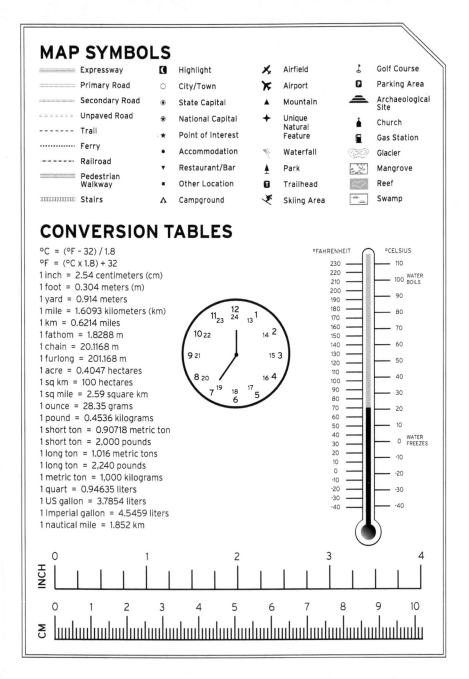

°C = (°F − 32) / 1.8
°F = (°C x 1.8) + 32
1 inch = 2.54 centimeters (cm)
1 foot = 0.304 meters (m)
1 yard = 0.914 meters
1 mile = 1.6093 kilometers (km)
1 km = 0.6214 miles
1 fathom = 1.8288 m
1 chain = 20.1168 m
1 furlong = 201.168 m
1 acre = 0.4047 hectares
1 sq km = 100 hectares
1 sq mile = 2.59 square km
1 ounce = 28.35 grams
1 pound = 0.4536 kilograms
1 short ton = 0.90718 metric ton
1 short ton = 2,000 pounds
1 long ton = 1.016 metric tons
1 long ton = 2,240 pounds
1 metric ton = 1,000 kilograms
1 quart = 0.94635 liters
1 US gallon = 3.7854 liters
1 Imperial gallon = 4.5459 liters
1 nautical mile = 1.852 km

MOON CALGARY

Avalon Travel
a member of the Perseus Books Group
1700 Fourth Street
Berkeley, CA 94710, USA
www.moon.com

Editor: Shaharazade Husain
Series Manager: Kathryn Ettinger
Copy Editor: Jehan Seirafi
Graphics and Production Coordinator:
  Elizabeth Jang
Cover Designer: Kathryn Osgood
Map Editor: Albert Angulo
Cartographers: Kat Bennett, Albert Angulo

ISBN: 978-1-59880-554-3

Text © 2010 by Andrew Hempstead.
Maps © 2010 by Avalon Travel.
All rights reserved.

Front cover photo: lunchtime in downtown Calgary
© Nelugo | Dreamstime.com
Title page: Calgary Stampede © Tourism Calgary

Printed in the United States of America

ABOUT THE AUTHOR

Andrew Hempstead

As a travel writer and photographer, Andrew Hempstead has spent many years exploring, photographing, and writing about Canada. Andrew is a happy resident of Alberta, where he lives with his family in Banff. Andrew has traveled mountain highways and hiked countless trails in Canada, exploring new places and updating old favorites. He spends as much time as possible on the road, traveling incognito, experiencing the many and varied delights of the region just as his readers do.

Andrew has been writing since the late 1980s, when he left an established career in advertising and took off for Alaska, linking up with veteran travel writer Deke Castleman to research and update the fourth edition of Moon's guide to Alaska and the Yukon. Since then he has produced several Moon guidebooks to Canada, including British Columbia, Vancouver and Victoria, the Canadian Rockies, Alberta, Atlantic Canada, and Nova Scotia. He is also the author of *Moon Australia* and *Moon New Zealand*, and a contributor to *Moon San Juan Islands, Road Trip USA, Northwest Best Places,* and *Eyewitness Guide to the USA,* as well as the updater of *The Illustrated Guide to New Zealand.* His writing and photographs have appeared in a wide variety of other media, including *National Geographic Traveler, Travesias, Where, Interval World,* Microsoft's *Automap,* and on the Alaska Airlines and Expedia websites.

The website www.westerncanadatravel.com showcases Andrew's work, while also providing invaluable planning tips for travelers heading to Canada.